I'm Excited About
Colossians

I'M EXCITED ABOUT COLOSSIANS

LIVING AND GROWING IN CHRIST IN A HOSTILE WORLD

PETER WADE

POSITIVE
WORD
MINISTRIES

Positive Word Ministries Inc.,
P.O. Box 115, Seaford SA 5169, Australia
Web site: **www.PeterWade.com**

ISBN: 978-0-909362-34-8

The author prefers to use an essentially literal translation of the Bible, in the King James Version tradition. Bible quotations in this book are based on the framework of the King James Version, modernized and with added insights gleaned from many sources over decades. Phrases quoted from other translations are identified and are copyright to their respective owners.

The material in this book was first taught by the author in June–September 1985, and was committed to writing in the Positive Words email newsletter from 2005-08. It has been completely revised by the author (2010).

Version 1.0

Religion / Christianity / Spiritual Life

My thanks to:

Vivien Wade, my co-laborer for over a half of a century;

Geri Johnson, for her typing skills in interpreting the spoken word;

Guy Vieira, who lovingly designed the cover and advised me on this book;

All my proof-readers who were invaluable;

and supporters of this ministry who have made this book a reality.

Contents

First Words

Paul's letter to the Colossians takes us to the heights of revealed truth about Christ perhaps like no other New Testament book. While Ephesians lifts our minds to heavenly places in Christ, Colossians reveals to us Who holds the universe together—Christ Jesus. "The doctrine of the Person of Christ is here stated with greater precision and fulness than in any other of St. Paul's epistles" (Bishop J.B. Lightfoot). This letter should be required reading at least every two or three months, perhaps in different translations each time. It can be read in around 20 minutes but will seed a lifetime of truth and practice.

As I have prepared this work for publication, I have deliberately avoided giving it the look or feel of a commentary. Some may term it a "devotional commentary" but I see it is a journey of inspiration and exploration.

It is in the rare style of expository preaching, though purists would prefer to confine the teaching to the stated passage. I say "rare" because the prominent television preachers hardly ever stray from "topical" preaching—one topic per sermon, with a catchy title and a text as a launching pad, followed by what we termed in Bible College as the "hop, skip, and jump" method! While some subjects can only be covered by that kind of treatment, today's crop of preachers need to be reminded that the Bible was written in ordered sentences and each book covers many topics. The advantages of reading and teaching a book in the order it was written are that believers actually learn what the book is about, and every subject that comes up has to be addressed without bias.

In editing this book for publication, it became obvious that I could not give an attribution for many of my sources. This material was developed as a series while I was a pastor of a local fellowship, and in the busy life of the pastorate I only made sufficient notes to jog my memory when I stood at the podium. I was trained to condense my notes to one page only, preferably no larger than half a letter or A4 page. If I didn't know my subject well enough, then I should not be preaching it!

I searched my memory and my library and can see traces of some headings coming from Warren Wiersbe's *Be Complete* and accompanying leader's guide with overhead slides, which I have used. I also see Wuest's *Word Studies in the Greek New Testament* on my shelves and *The Church Epistles* by E.W. Bullinger, along with standard reference works. In editing this material I have access on my computer to all the classic reference works and many translations. Since there is nothing new under the sun, I give thanks to those who have gone before and shared their understandings of the Word to all believers.

May you too be "excited about Colossians" and may it become one of your favorite books in God's positive Word.

1

Colossal Colossians!

Colossians 1:1-2

You *can* live and grow in Christ in a hostile world. To live God's way today you need a stable person resident in your life, and that person is Christ. You cannot live a fulfilled life without Christ. I know that there are many books written about positive living that will tell you otherwise, but I believe that so long as you have that empty gap within yourself that only God can fill, you will not live a positive life. Without Him we just *"drifted along on the stream of this world's ideas of living"* (Ephesians 2:2 Phillips). With Him we can do all things. With Him we have fantastic possibilities, and the colossal book of Colossians emphasizes the place of Christ in our lives.

It is interesting to note that Paul never went to Colossae. He did one trip through the area north of the city, but as far as the Bible record is concerned he never visited the city. So he introduces himself as an apostle, since he is writing to a group of people he has never met but about which he has heard much. He is currently under house arrest in Rome, and it is possible he may never get to meet them.

There is an interesting relationship between Ephesus and

Colossae; Ephesus is on the coast and Colossae about a hundred miles inland to the east. Acts 19:10 reveals that when Paul stayed at Ephesus for two years, the word of God reached all Asia [Minor], and one of the cities that it reached was Colossae. The believer who actually took the word of God there was a man named Epaphras (Colossians 1:7), who sat at Paul's feet, learned the truth, and then took it home and started what became a powerful and positive church in Colossae, as well as churches in the nearby cities of Laodicea and Hierapolis. All three cities were destroyed by an earthquake around 62 A.D.

Ephesians teaches that the believer is in Christ, while Colossians focuses on the Christ that is in the believer. E.W. Bullinger wrote that three-quarters (78) of the 95 verses in Colossians have a marked resemblance to verses in Ephesians (*The Church Epistles,* 2nd ed., 1905, p.175). It is therefore not surprising to see that while "in Christ" in various forms is used 35 times in Ephesians, it is also used 17 times in Colossians, for the truths of "in Christ" and "Christ in" have a vital relationship with each other. *Ephesians* *Colossians*

"*Paul, an apostle of Christ Jesus by the will of God, and Timothy our brother...*" (Colossians 1:1). You may have noticed a difference from the King James and other versions which read "Paul, an apostle of Jesus Christ." The Greek texts use the form "Christ Jesus" in this verse, not "Jesus Christ". What is the difference? Am I any different if I am called Peter Wade or if I am called Wade Peter? Sometimes computer login names have your last name first and then your Christian name or initial, but you are still you. The difference between "Christ Jesus" and "Jesus Christ" is a difference in emphasis.

10

(There are around a dozen different titles given to Christ in the New Testament.) If Paul was named an apostle of Jesus Christ, the emphasis would be upon the earthly Jesus, the one who was humiliated, the one who was crucified, and who later became the risen, victorious Christ. If Paul was named an apostle of Christ Jesus, then the emphasis is on the risen, victorious Christ who had been humiliated. There is a great difference between those two concepts. Do we worship the the humanity of the Lord, the Jesus of the beard and the sandals? Do we worship the Jesus crucified on the cross? Or do we worship Christ Jesus who sits at the right hand of God in the heavenlies, the powerful, victorious, overcoming one? You have to ask yourself those questions. I worship Christ Jesus, the victorious Son of God. I'm thankful for everything Jesus did for me upon the cross, but I've found in the Bible that God carefully uses words and when He speaks in the revelation to Paul of what He has done for me, it's always the finished work of the victorious Christ Jesus that is in view.

Colossians is written *"to the saints and the faithful brothers in Christ in Colossae: ..."* (verse 2a). Not all saints are faithful. A saint in Bible terms is simply a Christian believer. It is not a person who has been canonized by the church years after they have died. A saint is simply a person who believes in God and has accepted Christ as their Savior. There will always be saints, and there will always be faithful brothers and sisters. There are those who may have become believers but have not developed further. And there are those who recognize their place in the family of God, and want to maximize their potential as a child of God, and see the kingdom of God extended. They are the faithful brethren in Christ.

"Grace to you and peace from God our Father and the Lord Jesus Christ" (verse 2b). Grace or favour signifies all the blessings we have in Christ and is often used throughout the Bible, while peace comes directly from the Hebrew greeting of Shalom. The combination of grace and peace is often used in salutations in Paul's writings. Some believe grace was the term for the Gentiles while peace was the greeting to the Jews.

2

Christian, You are Unique!

Colossians 1:3-5

When I am reading verses 3 to 8, the question comes to me, "If this were the only document I had about the Christian faith, what would I know about being a Christian from this?" I think this is an interesting way to look at it. If I was living in Colossae and I had no other documents apart from the Old Testament in the synagogue, that is, no other New Testament documents, what would this tell me about a Christian? Could I tell anything from this as to who is a Christian, what is their potential, and so on? And I believe we can, so let's look at it for a moment. This will also start us on our quest to *get the basics straight*—what is a Christian and who is this Christ?

The first thing we discover is that a Christian is someone **who knows God exists**, as it says in Hebrews 11:6, and that He rewards those who seek Him. A Christian knows that God exists. A Christian is one who has faith in the invisible. We will probably never see God in this life, but He is here and He is as real to us as our spouses, our mothers and fathers, and the rest of the people with whom we rub shoulders. God is just that real to a Christian. This is an important point to recognize. We can easily forget it sometimes. We see our friends and our family so often and we do not question that they are real. We need to get to the same place of recognizing that God is just as real, just as certain as the people we can see.

In verse 3 Paul says, *"We give thanks to God and the Father of our Lord Jesus Christ, praying always for you."* You do not give thanks to someone whom you do not believe exists. A Christian is a person who knows that God is worthy to receive our thanks for everything. *"God... the Father of our Lord Jesus Christ"*—there's another whole study here as to how God describes himself. The one name that God delights in calling himself is the "Father of our Lord Jesus Christ". (See Colossians 3:17, and also Romans 15:6, II Corinthians 1:3 and 11:31, and I Peter 1:3.) God is a very proud father. He loves to call Himself the Father of our Lord Jesus Christ.

Another thing we can find out about a Christian is given in verse 4, *"since we heard of your faith in Christ Jesus."* A Christian is one *who has faith in Christ Jesus*. That is God's own definition. There is a relationship between a Christian and Christ. A lot of people talk about God but who or what are they talking about? Is it just the First Cause, the Supreme Being? Many religions use the word "God". Allah, the moon God, is not the Father of our Lord Jesus Christ. Buddha is not the God who saved us. A Christian by definition is one who has faith in, believes in, Christ Jesus. The central person of the Christian religion is Christ, the son of God. That is really important to keep in your mind. *or God*

So a Christian is a person who really believes in Christ. He doesn't go around saying, "Whenever I'm in trouble I talk to the man upstairs." Believing in Christ is different from just talking to the man upstairs when you get into trouble. To believe means to lean your whole weight upon the object of your belief. Christ is the center of my life. In fact, later on in this chapter we will read that He's living in me (verse 27), and He's living through me (3:4). The center of everything to do with the Christian life is Christ. And as believers we have come to faith in Christ.

It is important to see how God works on a person to embrace faith in Christ. There are steps to having faith in Christ. God first works on the mind. You see, everybody has a mind, and God works on that mind so that as we hear the gospel, the Good News; we take a seed of truth and think about it. We are told that there are 10,000 messages a day coming into your brain through your sight and through your hearing. God gets to people first through their mind. That's why we share the Good News. That is why we give out leaflets and books and have web sites. That is why we say the right word at the right time. God gets a person's attention and they hear and understand the Good News. They learn that God has only the best for them.

Then there's another step that He takes. Emotion is involved. I can take facts into my mind about my computer and how it works. I don't get emotional unless the computer doesn't work. Then I have been known to get emotional! But the fact itself is not an emotional thing. Sales people are taught to sell the sizzle and not the steak! When it comes to the Good News, then I see there is a glorious future for me. God has done so much for me, and He drops a small picture of the benefit into my mind, and then my emotions get stirred up. I have a desire to get hold of this good life that God is talking about. There's a certain expectation that comes

The sizzle!

Jews still waiting for Messiah — accept Jesus but look at Jesus' promise to me. Elvis Presley said he did not understand his mother's faith but he wanted it! A lot of people go about witnessing as if they were prosecuting attorneys. They just want to tell people what miserable sinners they are and how they are on the road to Hell. However, the way to encourage folk to join the family of God is to tell them how good God is. Hold out the carrot! Make them see that this life you're talking about is not a life of giving up something. It's a life of receiving something better than you have right now. And that starts desire happening in the emotions.

Then we're ready to go one step further and we make an act of the will and commit our life to Christ. You might have noticed there—the mind, the emotions, and the will. They comprise what we call the soul of a person. You have a mind; you have emotions; and you have a will. And it's your will that decides what you are going to do. Having taken in the Good News, having got the desire and expectation that you want what God is offering, then you will to have it. You say, "I will go God's way and I will commit my life to Christ." When you do that you will receive God's spiritual gift package. That is how we get to faith in Christ. It always works that way. God goes through the mind first. Your emotions then get involved, and there follows an act of your will. You do not become a Christian by being born in a Christian country. You do not become a car by being born in a garage! You become a Christian by an act of the will, and from that moment you are "saved".

Let's go back to verse 4 again. *"Since we heard of your faith in Christ"*, so a Christian is one who believes in Christ. And then it says, *"and of the love that you have for all the saints."* Christians are people *who love each other*. Now it's getting difficult. You mean I have to love all the Christians? I mean to say, have you met some of the ones I've run across? Someone wrote this oft-quoted verse:

> To live above with saints we love,
> Will certainly be glory.
> To live below with saints we know,
> Well that's another story!

Christians are people who love each other. That's another Bible definition of a Christian (John 13:35, Romans 13:8, etc.). A Christian is one who is not thinking of themselves but of somebody else. That has to be the hallmark of Christianity. And that is the way that you get answers to your problems. When you quit thinking about what a terrible mess you are making of life and you start thinking about somebody else's problem, then you find you start getting answers to your own challenges. If you think your problem is more than you can bear, come visit with me and I'll take you around the hospital one time and I think we can solve that attitude fairly quickly. A Christian is noted as one who thinks about others before they think about themselves.

A Christian, it says in verse 4, is one who has love for *all* the saints. We've already seen that truth in verse 2 and the word "saints" is used again in verse 4. A Christian is one *who has a good self-image.* In Bible terms, a saint is one who belongs to the family of God. A saint is one who has Christ in them, the hope of glory. A saint is a member of God's family. That is why I get upset and even express myself strongly at times when people say they are "only a sinner saved by grace". That is not what God says you are. Certainly you *were* a sinner. Certainly you *were* saved by grace. But what are you *now?* You are a saint. You are a son or

17

daughter in God's family. Christian, you must have a good self-image. Those Christians who seem so spiritual when they say they are "only sinners saved by grace" may sound humble but it is not true. I was a sinner but now I'm a saved person. We need to say, "I know who I am. I am a child of God with power." Let's have a good, healthy self-image. A Christian knows God. He or she believes in Christ, and has love to all the saints. He or she has a good self-image.

Verse 5 states that a Christian is one *who has expectation*. *"Because of the expectation laid up for you in heaven."* I believe the word "hope" (KJV) should always be translated "expectation". God has an expectation which is stored away for you in heaven. God has placed your name on it, its gift-wrapped ready for you to take into your life and enjoy the benefit of it. There is expectation in the Christian life. I'm so glad I'm a Christian, and I'm glad I have an expectation for the future. Yesterday I was listening to a tape where the speaker asked "How should we handle the book of Revelation and what effect does it have on us?" He took the same approach that I do. He basically said that if you think you are going to go through those things, then you are in the wrong family. If you are in God's family, the book of Revelation is not for you—you'll be gone! But if you are not in God's family, then you had better brace yourself because there are some things coming that you may not like.

3

The Power of the Gospel

Colossians 1:5-8

I am continuing to help you discover what a Christian really is.
In the second half of verse 5 and then verse 6 it states *"in which
you heard before in the word of the truth, the gospel, ⁶which has
come to you, just as also in all the world, and is bearing fruit and
growing, just as also among you, from the day which you heard and
fully knew the grace of God in truth"*. We have a powerful manual
for everyday life in the word of truth, the gospel. A Christian is one
who has a roadmap for their future, and that is the Word of
God. This is another thing that separates a Christian from
everybody else. We have a love for one Book above all other books.
It is accurate when we are called the "people of the Book." When
we have a problem we go to the Bible, because it's the book that
gives the answers to our problem.

There's another fact I want to share. The King James Version
in verse 6 merely says that this word of truth "bringeth forth fruit".
Almost all the modern translations will add "and is growing" or
"increases it" or similar. For some reason the King James Version
has failed to translate a Greek word there. So we should read *"it
is bearing fruit and growing"* (as in verse 10 also). "Bearing" and

19

"growing" are in the middle voice, both acting and acted upon, a combination of the English active and passive voices.

In verse 6 it states that is the gospel, the word of the truth (previous verse), that is doing the work. The word of truth bears fruit and is growing. It is an action taken to and for itself. The object is the word of truth. That means that the good news you share with somebody is a very powerful thing, and has inherent within it the capability of reproduction, just like a seed. A seed has within it a program, a pattern. It is better than a computer program, because it lasts for thousands of years and it does the same thing every time. It reproduces itself according to a pattern. Every acorn has the capability of becoming an oak tree. It will never become a fir tree or a eucalyptus tree, because it is programmed by God to reproduce as an oak tree.

The word of the truth, the good news, has within itself the capability of reproducing itself and growing, and so it perpetually continues on. I believe that the gospel is far greater than anybody yet conceives. I've seen it happen in the lives of people who were just nominal Christians, that is, they probably went to church when they were children and then later they forgot all about God and church, or they belong to a church but do not express their faith in everyday life. However, when they have heard "the word of the truth", they have been saved and made a commitment to Christ, simply because of what they have heard. There may not have been an altar call, a "walking of the aisle" to the front of the church for prayer, or any outward action, but they are now saved. That is how powerful the gospel is that we share. God never told us to tell people what miserable sinners they are. Most people already know that. God wants us to tell them how good He is, and how He made a perfect sacrifice so every person can become a member of His family.

So we share the good news, and as that good news goes out, gradually people start believing it and make their commitment. Then they start applying the principles in God's Word. Some have sat under this teaching for four or five years and then gradually they grasp the principles and accept what God says about their lives. I've seen many people drop off bad habits, not because I have made snide remarks about them, which I try not to do, but because it is the Word of God that does the work. People come to church with their hurts, habits, and hangups, and it's the word of the truth that has the answers to all those situations.

*"The word of the truth, the gospel, *6*which has come to you, just as also in all the world, and is bearing fruit and growing, just as also among you, from the day which you heard and fully knew* [or realized] *the grace of God in truth"* (verses 5b and 6). What a powerful truth this good news is! What a great work it does in the lives of people! No wonder Paul wrote to the Romans, *"The gospel... is the power of God unto salvation to everyone who believes"* (1:16). One of the great secrets of living and growing in Christ in a hostile world is to get your foundation right. The foundation we have is the good news of what God reveals about us. It is the good news of what a Christian is—one who knows God and believes in Christ. That is why I am spending this time in the colossal book of Colossians, to strengthen the foundation so that you too can live a victorious life. It is not just a matter of reading the book. It's thinking about the word of the truth, drilling it into your

consciousness, so that if anything negative ever happens you say, "That's not what God says about me." You know who you are. You are a saint—a son of God or a daughter of God with power. You know where you are going when you die, and that is to be with Christ for eternity. You know what's important to you, and that is to have knowledge of what God says about you, so you are sure about what you can do. That's where it makes a difference. You can live God's way in a negative world.

Then in verse 7 it says the Christian is one *who is a learner. "Just as you learned from Epaphras, our beloved fellow servant."* The word "learned" is from the same Greek root word as the word "disciple." We need to be learners. We need to see ourselves in school. To me the church is not a first-aid station where you put a band-aid on people's problems and send them out to struggle in the world for another week. My model of the church is as an educational institution. We are all learners in the school of Christ. We need to take that position as a learner. There is so much to learn and I'm still learning more as I go along. I've been teaching for over half a century and I'm still learning truth in passages that I've gone through time and time again.

A Christian is a learner. There is a learning process that goes on. When we were non-Christians we first heard the good news, for without hearing the good news we could never become a Christian. Once we heard the good news, we believe in Christ, and having believed in Christ we become learners, disciples. Right now you are learning something about the Bible. As learners we grow in our knowledge of Christ, and soon we learn that we became a Christian in order that we may bear fruit. The fruit that we produce is to share the good news with somebody else. And so the cycle goes over and over, and this is how God's kingdom is extended. This is how we bring new children into the family of God. We hear the good news. We believe in Christ. We are then learners. We learn what we need to know as fruit-bearing plants in His vineyard. (Spread Good news)

Continuing with verse 7 and then 8, we read of Epaphras, the "faithful minister" of the Colossian church. *"Just as you learned from Epaphras, our beloved fellow servant, who is a faithful minister of Christ for you, [8]who also told us of your love in the Spirit."* We will come across Epaphras again in the letter to Philemon, discussed at the end of this book. Epaphras is also mentioned in Colossians 4:12, where it is implied he was in Rome with Paul, encouraging him and ministering to him.

Faith, hope, love

I want to go back over these first few verses of chapter one just briefly, because there are some other things we need to see there. Put a circle around the word "faith" in verse 4. And put a circle around the word "love" in verse 4. And put another one around the word "hope" in verse 5. Those circles might help bring to your mind three great abiding things: faith, love, and hope. These are mentioned many times in the New Testament, and several times as a group of three. The most well-known example would be in I Corinthians 13:13, *"And now abide faith, hope, and love, these three; yet the greatest of these is love."* That particular passage puts them in a different order to what we have here in Colossians, while I Thessalonians 1:3 and 5:8 follow the same order as Colossians. These are very important concepts. Faith,

Faith, Hope, Love

love, and hope. A Christian is one who has those three concepts operating in their lives.

We must explore our terms. How does faith come? The Bible says faith comes by hearing, *"So faith comes from hearing, and hearing through the message about Christ"* (Romans 10:17). What do we do with faith? We *"walk by faith"* (II Corinthians 5:7). So we not only become a Christian by faith, but we walk in the Christian life by faith. Then there is our *"work of faith"* (I Thessalonians 1:3). Faith is such an integral part of the Christian life that without it there is no Christian life. We pray in faith to an invisible God that hears and works miracles on our behalf.

Then love. How do we get love? Romans 5:5 says, *"The love of God has been poured out in our hearts through the Holy Spirit given to us."* So God's love is now resident within us. It's not regular human love; it's the love which only God can give. *"Agape"* love is the word in the Bible. It's a love that embraces the whole world. We can love the unlovely. General William Booth, founder of the Salvation Army, often said, "Go for souls and go for the worst." It is necessary often to love someone who is unlovely from our viewpoint in order to bring them into the family of God. And, of course, we not only need to go for the worst we must also go for the best. God loves the "up and outs" as much as the "down and outs". They all need the same great message of truth. In addition, our love one to another is our greatest expression of that love.

What is hope or expectation? Hope is something the world does not have. If you believe what is recorded in the book of Revelation, you will know how true that is. Our hope, our expectation comes through the cross of Christ, for it is only Christ

People Created to

love, glory

try us

Things loved

Glen Bird
6-12-14
(Really Paul)

that gives expectation to us. This is not a "wishy-washy hope-so, maybe" situation. It is very much a sure, solid thing. We live out the positive expectation of our hope. If you believe that tomorrow the thing you started to do would prosper and be an enormous success, how would you look? You would dress yourself up to the hilt. You would let the world know that you are on top of the situation and you are in control, and it is going to work out beautifully to your benefit and help others as well. That's what expectation does for you. That's why I'm excited about being a Christian.

You are included

Let's look back at the first eight verses yet again. I want you to see how often you get a mention. You are mentioned for you are included in the word "you." First, "Grace to *you*", verse 2. "We pray for *you*", verse 3, verse 4, it's "*your* faith", and "the love that *you* have for all the saints." Verse 5, "The expectation laid up for *you*", and "the word of the truth... which has come to *you*", verses 5b and 6. "And it is bearing fruit and growing... among *you*", verse 6. And then "just as *you* learned [the grace of God in truth]...", verses 6b and 7. "Epaphras... a faithful minister of Christ for *you*... has made known to us *your* love in the spirit", verses 7 and 8. Can you see how God is pointing out these truths right at you and me? Can you get the message from that? It is really personal what God has done for us. It is tremendous.

4

A Christian's Positive Goals

Colossians 1:9-10

In this section of Colossians the emphasis is on a Christian's positive goals, and we continue in chapter one and verse 9. The first word in verse 9 is the word "for" or "and" in some translations, so we know that what we are going to discover is based on the description of a Christian that was given in the first part of chapter one.

Let me first point out the important difference between being complete and being mature. The difference is well illustrated by an acorn and an oak tree. An acorn is complete. It has within it a program, if we put it in computer terms, that ensures every acorn placed in the right situation will produce an oak tree. It never produces a fir tree. It never produces an orange tree. An acorn always produces an oak tree. Wrapped up within that hard little shell is an oak tree wanting to reach for the sky, and when the acorn is placed in the ground, and water and warmth are available, the tree grows to maturity. I believe a Christian, from the moment he or she is born again, is complete. That is what the Bible teaches. We're going to come across this clearly later in Colossians. A Christian is complete in reality, in spirit, and potentially in every other part of their being. What God wants is for us to be complete in maturity.

Let's see how it shows itself in the life of a Christian as he or she develops. First, he discovers "Christ for him" (Romans 5:8) and this is the point of salvation. He realizes and accepts "Christ died for him." Then as he understands the Word more, he recognizes that he has "Christ in him" (Colossians 1:27), and so the original concept of salvation grows to something larger and he realizes that he is a walking container of Christ. That is what a Christian is: Christ in a person. And yet there is one more stage to go, and that is when he sees "Christ as him" (Colossians 3:4). Christ is in every part of his being and his only life is to live out the life of Christ in the world. That is where we're heading in the book of Colossians.

So we come to verse 9 and read what God has to say to us, as I look at a Christian's positive goals. *"For this cause we also, from the day we heard, have not ceased to pray for you, asking that you may be filled with the knowledge of his will in all spiritual wisdom and understanding."* What a powerful verse! That little word "all" is an incredible word. It appears some thirty times in the book of Colossians. In fact, it would be a good exercise to just mark or underline every time the word "all" or "every" is present and see its impact in what God is saying to us. The first goal that a positive Christian has is to be filled with, or better to *be filled full of, the knowledge of God's will*. That is my goal—to so know God's will for my life that I can fulfill it and accomplish it. The concept of being filled appears some seven times in Colossians, because God sees us not just as people who have a ticket to heaven but as people filled with Christ, filled with the knowledge of his will, and filled with His power and many other things.

I often tell people about my good friend Ky Eshelman from Covington, Ohio. She was a rather large lady, the kind of person my Dad used to say in the old days, "Once round her and twice around the local lighthouse!" That was just a figure of speech to show some impact of mass. Ky was a wonderful, bubbly Christian. She would go up to people she was meeting for the first time and say, "I'm loaded and expecting", and they would look at this large figure and get all kinds of thoughts from that statement. Then she would say, "The Bible says in Psalms that he daily loads me with benefits, and I'm expecting his return at any time."

So see yourself as loaded and expecting. This prayer, this goal for the Christians is that they might be filled full with the knowledge of his will. This is a deep knowledge. This is a realization of his will in their lives. This is possible, and that's the key that we must get into our minds. It is possible to know what God wants you to do in life. Isn't that incredible? The God and Father of our Lord Jesus Christ, the Almighty God who made heaven and earth, wants you to know what He has specifically planned for your life. We can be filled full with the knowledge of his will. Of course, once we are filled full of it then we can fulfill it, we can bring it to pass in our lives. That is a very positive goal.

There is another goal in verse ten, and that is to live a life worthy of the Christ within. It says, "That you should walk worthy of the Lord, fully pleasing to him in every good work, bearing fruit and increasing in the full knowledge of God." The word "walk" in the New Testament usually means the manner of life, the way you live your life. So we could read, "That you might live your life worthy, of like value, as the Lord." God's goal for you and me is that our lives should be worth as much as the life of Christ was to this world. Can you take that in? It's hard, isn't it? It's an incredible concept. God wants your life to have a similar impact upon the world as the life of Jesus Christ did. The only way that can happen is if you live out the Christ life within you.

I Peter 2:21 has something to say that might help us to understand this Colossian verse better. *"For to this you were called, because Christ also suffered for you, leaving you an example, that you might follow in his steps."* He left us an example that we should follow his steps. If we follow the example, then we can live out the Christ life in this world and the world will sit up and take notice that here is a person who knows Christ, who has Christ's qualities and characteristics in them.

If you want to know what Christ is like, a good place to start is to read Matthew, Mark, Luke, and John. A summary of his earthly ministry is given in Acts 10:38, *"God anointed Jesus of Nazareth with the Holy Spirit and with power, who went about doing good and healing all who were oppressed by the devil, for God was with him."* The same God that was with Christ is with you and with me. That means we can go out and do good. What was the good that Jesus did? He healed those who were oppressed. He found a need and filled it. He found a hurt and healed it. Where there was a need for supply, he supplied it. Where there was a need for health, he removed the blockage and let it flow. Where there was a need to bring two people together, he brought them together. Christ was there among humanity, helping people

29

maximize their potential. And we can do the same. A life worthy, of the same value, as Christ; we can live it because He showed us how it could be done. One of the problems you and I have in the natural is that we are trying to do something that's never been done—to live out our unique lives. When you look at it from the human level, that is really something. But when you look at it from the Christian level, we don't need to attempt to live out our lives. We need to live out His life, and that makes life an experience with no stress or strain.

Living out His life produces a positive result—"*bearing fruit*" (verse 10). There is no better work in being fruitful than to share the good news with other people. Tell them the good news, and bring them into the family. Lead them to enjoy the same benefits as you do. There are other works that are good, and you can think of those that fit your particular situation. To be fruitful shows growth. God wants you to grow. He wants you to develop your ability to help others. This is the principle of giving and receiving. You give a little time to help somebody else. You do a small act to help them and it will come back to you. This week on television there was a report of somebody who had a terrible debilitating handicap that was really very difficult. The way they received their healing was to take their eyes off the problem and start helping somebody else. And when they did that, they were healed. Again, what is that? The principle of giving and receiving. Get your eyes off yourself, get them on someone else, and then watch the blessings flow back in. That is beautiful.

Verse 10 continues, "*and increasing in the full knowledge of God*" or "*growing in the realization of God*" (Concordant).

We start off as seeing the God Who sent His Son to die for us. Then we see Him further as a father figure and we realize that we are in a relationship. That relationship develops and we read the Bible more and discover that God is everywhere. Wherever you go, God is. There's no place you can go where He is not present. We rejoice in this immensity of God, and then we read the Bible even further and see that it is God in Christ in me. Now we really appreciate God in a great measure. That is what we are doing week by week, day by day. The more we hear and read the Word of God, the more we grow in the knowledge of God. If you don't think you're getting enough on Sunday mornings or in your weekly fellowship meeting, then "a verse a day will keep the devil away". Get some food during the week. You can't have one snack on Sunday morning and think you're going to last all week long— it just doesn't work that way. Get your teeth into the Book and grow in the knowledge, in the realization of God.

You might also notice three words in verses 9 and 10— "wisdom," "walk," and "work." Mark them in your Bible. That is the divine order. First discover God's wisdom, know what God says about the situation, then you can walk on the basis of it and produce the work, the fruit God wants for you. You cannot change the order. If you want the fruit you must tap into God's wisdom first. That is the cycle and that is how we grow and increase in God. What a powerful, positive goal for the Christian! What is a goal? It has been defined a hundred ways in these days of success philosophy. We need to be careful that a goal doesn't become a rut. Someone said a goal is a moving target. I like that because my goals for this year are different from what my goals need to be for next year. My goals need to increase and grow as I increase and grow. A goal needs to be a moving target, and as we take in God's wisdom we increase our goals and so we grow further.

5

More Positive Goals

Colossians 1:11-14

In verse 11 is another positive goal for the Christian. *"Being strengthened with all power, according to the might of His glory, unto all endurance and patience with joy."* Let's start with the first phrase of the verse—*"strengthened with all power"*. The Greek word for "strengthened" is from the root word "dunamis", from which we get the English word "dynamo." The power in a dynamo ("generator" is the preferred modern word) is not power that you can measure or feel or see until the dynamo starts turning. I have illustrated this previously in my book on Ephesians, and for the sake of completeness I will use the same illustration here. As a boy I had a dynamo on the fork of my bicycle, known as a bottle or sidewall dynamo. When I lifted a lever, the wheel on the top of the dynamo came in contact with the side of the tire, and as I pedalled the front and back lights came on. This is potential power, like the power in the car battery. One of the cars we owned had a great setup. When you got out of the car and locked the door, the interior light stayed on. My wife or I would walk away and get up to the front step of our house, yet the light was still on in the car. We would hesitate, turn around to go back to the car to turn the light off, and then it turned itself off. It had a mind of its own, or so it seemed until we became accustomed to it. Wonderful things, these modern cars! The car's battery has potential power, and when I walked out the next day and put the key in the lock and opened the door, the light came back on again. The potential power was there all the time just waiting for me to do something. That is how the power of God is in our lives.

The prayer is for us to be "strengthened with all power"—to be powered with all His power. We are powerful, dynamic people walking through life, and God is waiting for us to get the negative and the positive together so the power does something worthwhile. Note the order: to be filled, to be fruitful, to be forti-fied (William MacDonald). The order is important. *"Strengthened with all power, according to..."*—the law of standard (F.E. Marsh). According to what? According to our needs? No. It is according to the source—*"the might* [or strength] *of His glory."* "Might" here is the Greek word "kratos," perfect strength. In the New Testament it is applied only to God. It is God's power in action. So we have potential power, and its measure is according to the power of God that is in operation in this universe—that is tremendous power. In fact, Ephesians 1:19-20 tells us that it is the same power that God used to raise Jesus Christ from the dead and set Him at his own right hand!

Now, why do we have this power? It says in verse 11 b, *"for all endurance and patience with joy"*. The word "endurance" means "remaining under difficulties without succumbing" (Robertson). It is patience or longsuffering in respect to things and circumstances. It is patience in respect of trials. How often we get impatient with the speed at which things happen! Patience, knowing that the sun is going to come up tomorrow morning and it will be another whole day untouched when we can work on that particular situation. What we need to do is to operate God's power to produce that patience—a patient endurance is spoken of here.

"Longsuffering" (KJV) is a good word. It has to do with people. There are some people we suffer long. Yes, we all have them. Yet we have God's power within us and using that power we can say, "Father, I can't put up with this person any longer. I need your help," and that is when help floods in to get you through that situation. In fact, it helps you so much that it says that we can have both endurance and patience "with joy." That's a good way of handling your enemies, isn't it? Endurance and patience with joyfulness. You get excited about it as you see God at work in the situation. So one of my positive goals as a Christian is to manifest God's power in respect of things and people, so I can handle life's situations God's way. I believe you and I can handle them if we recognize that we are loaded with the power of God.

One final goal given to the Christian in this passage is found in verses 12 to 14. *"Giving thanks to the Father..."* A Christian's positive goal is *to be thankful,* and first to thank God. "The attitude of gratitude" as someone has called it. We need to be thankful for everything in life. *"In everything give thanks"* (Philippians 4:6). When you are in a fix, look up Philippians 4:6. You might be sick or have a financial shortage, but it says, *"in everything give thanks."* That's quite a difference. *"Giving thanks always for all things"* (Ephesians 5:20). When God says "all things" you can study Greek until you are blue in the face and "all things" will still mean "all things!" There is no modifier to the word "all."

One preacher told of the time a thief stole his wallet out of his pocket, and he said, "Well, praise God." His companion said, "What are you praising God for?" And he started listing things that he could praise God for "in" that situation. He praised God that the man only took his wallet and didn't take his life. That's a good thing to praise God for! He praised God that it was God who was the supply of his need and not his wallet, and his life would go along with or without his wallet. So it does not matter what situation you are in—get your eyes off the situation and get them on God. And the best way to do that is to praise God. If you can find nothing to praise "in" the situation, at least praise God for Who He is. That's a good place to start. And when you do, you will get the situation into perspective and His peace and guidance will flow to you.

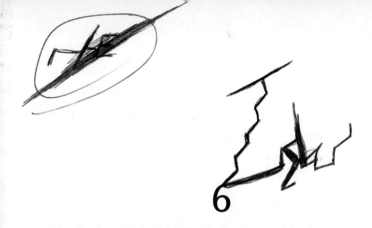

6

Four Subjects for Thanksgiving

Colossians 1:12-14

In verses 12 to 14 we have four things for which we should be thankful. *"Giving thanks to the Father, who has qualified you to share in the inheritance of the saints in the light, 13Who has rescued us out from the authority of darkness and transferred us into the kingdom of his beloved Son, 14in whom we have redemption, the forgiveness of sins."*

First, *"Giving thanks to the Father, who has qualified you to share in the inheritance of the saints in the light."* We are qualified or **rendered fit**—*"rendered fit to enjoy the inheritance"*. We were rendered fit by accepting Jesus as Lord and Savior. We accepted Him as the Lord of our lives, and He did the qualifying for the inheritance! It is nothing you did or could do. You are not saved by your works. You are not saved by your good looks. You are not saved because you live on the right side of the tracks. You are saved only because Christ died for you. God qualified you for all the blessings that He has available. Isn't that exciting? You are qualified! Now that's something to give thanks to God for. Be thankful for being qualified to share in the inheritance.

Ephesians 1:14 states that what we now have is only the down-payment, the earnest, "the portion" (Amplified). We all know what down-payments are. If what I now have is only the down-payment, what the total is going to be I just cannot comprehend fully. The Word says that the down-payment means that I have total health. I have total financial independence in God. I have total ability to relate to every person I run across. I have total power within me to handle every situation in life. That is just the down payment—just the 10%, if you want to put it that way. What is the total going to be? We'll find out when we get to heaven, but I'm just enjoying the down-payment at the moment. Are you?

Then what else are we to be thankful for? Verse 13 teaches *"Who has rescued us out from the authority of darkness."* The word "delivered" (KJV) is *"rescued"*—"He has rescued us" (CEV, CLV, CSB, NLT, etc.). From what? From the authority or domain of darkness. We are rescued persons. God knew that we needed help, just the same as if you saw a person fall on the road in front of a bus, you would rush to pull them out of harm's way. That's what God did for us. He saw that we had real problems, so he sent Jesus to make the way legally available for us to be rescued from the domain of darkness—those negative situations where everything always goes wrong, from that power of darkness controlled by Satan who wants to drag you down. We have been rescued from that. Give thanks!

Yet there's more for which we are to be thankful. He didn't just drag us from out of the darkness and leave us lying on the sidewalk or the pavement. No, he *"transported* [transferred] *us into the kingdom of his beloved Son"* ("translated us", KJV). The word means to remove from one place to another. He *removed* us, so we are no longer in the domain of darkness. We have been removed into the kingdom of his beloved Son or the kingdom of the Son of his love. We have been taken out of the governmental control of darkness that just dragged us down, and we have been transferred into God's kingdom. That's something to give God thanks for!

Verse 14 gives the fourth initiative for thanksgiving. *"In whom we have redemption, the forgiveness of sins."* (The words "through his blood" [KJV] are omitted by all the early Greek texts and most modern translations. We know it is through his blood from other passages, but it is not mentioned here.) *"Redemption"* is the payment of a ransom for a slave or debtor. "He paid a debt he did not owe, I owed a debt I could not pay", as the popular chorus goes. The word "forgiveness" means release from our sins, remission of our sins. We are released from our sins, and that is a critical truth.

One reason why so many Christians live negative lives is that they do not recognize that they are not only released from the penalty of sin—which meant that they were going to Hell, to use evangelical terminology—but they are released from the power of sin. We just read in verse 13 that we have been rescued from the domain of darkness. Now we know that God has released us, not just from the fact that we will no longer have to pay for our sin but He has released us from the everyday power of that sin. We are totally released people. There is nothing hanging on in our lives that will drag us down anymore. I say nothing—there is left only whatever you want to hang on to in your mind. As far as God is concerned there is nothing, but some of us still want to hang on to this little bit or hang on to that little bit of the old life because we have not yet learned the joy of totally trusting God.

So, there are four things to give thanks for in verses 12 to 14: we've been rendered fit, rescued from the domain of darkness, removed into Christ's kingdom, and redeemed from the penalty and the power of sin. Those are very positive causes for thanksgiving. We are already complete. God wants us to work out that completeness in our lives and enjoy it. In Colossians one we have seen so far that He wants us filled full with the knowledge of God's will, we are to live the Christ life, be fruitful in reproduction and in good works, grow in the realization of God, manifest His power in relation to people as well as situations, and to be thankful for being rendered fit, rescued, removed and released. These are the first goals on the road to a happy life. Did you notice there is not a word about material possessions or pleasures? Why? Nothing wrong with those outward things, but these inward truths come first.

Matthew 6:33 says, *"But seek first the kingdom of God and his righteousness, and all these things will be added to you."* These are beautiful, powerful words of the Lord Jesus Christ. Get this area right and the rest will fall into place. "All these things will be added to you." What things? The things you need (verse 31)— what you eat, what you drink, what you wear. *"Your heavenly Father knows that you need all these things"* (verse 32b). Yet *"seek first the kingdom of God and His righteousness"* and all these things will be added to you.

I can remember as a young Christian reading a commentary by Adam Clarke on this passage and he illustrated it by quoting a Mr. Trapp. "They shall be cast in as an overplus, or as small advantages to the main bargain; as paper and pack-thread are given where we buy spice and fruit..." He is saying it is like when you go to the supermarket and you want some apples. You select the apples and put them in a paper or plastic bag, so you go home not only with the apples but also with a paper bag. The paper bag or sack is the thing that's been added to you. We can understand this better these days because many people buy a particular jar of honey or peanut butter or whatever, because of the fancy jar. They want the jar, and along with the jar happens to come the peanut butter or the honey.

The early church fathers, Clement, Origen, and Eusebius, added these words as the words of Christ: "Ask great things, and little things shall be added unto you; ask heavenly things, and earthly things shall be added unto you." God is saying in verse 33, "You seek me and my kingdom, and the other necessary things will come along with it." It is all wrapped up in the spiritual gift package that God has given us. God has only the best for you— health, wealth, and happiness. That is His will for you, but you cannot have them unless you put His kingdom first. You must have a God-first consciousness and see yourself as a saint. Recognize that you have certain goals to grow in your realization of God, and all these things shall be added unto you.

7

Christ, first in everything

Colossians 1:15

I was involved in commercial publishing for a number of years, and there were always two types of non-fiction books close to the top of the bestseller lists. The top category was recipe books. I'm sure if I went into your house, I would find a collection of recipe books. The second type of books that people want to read is biographies, books about people. People always want to know about people—not only in books, but on television, in movies, and in magazines and newspapers. The more public a person is the more we want to know how they live their lives. Just what does the Queen do when she gets behind the walls of the Buckingham Palace? What does the presidential family do in the White House?

I think it's the same as we come to the Word of God. We want to know who is this Jesus. Just what was he really like? In order to understand Colossians chapter 1 and verse 15 onward, we must go back a little and briefly review where we've been already in chapter one. What we have to do if we are going to live and grow in Christ in a hostile world is to *get the basics straight,* and this is most important. What are the basics? The first basic truth is that the Christian is a unique person. There's something different about being a Christian. We found out that a Christian is one who loves God,. A Christian is one who has faith in Christ. A Christian is one who loves other people. A Christian is one who has a good self-image as a son and daughter of God. These facts are taught in verses one to eight of Colossians chapter one. Then secondly we saw that a Christian needs positive Christian goals. Our greatest goal is to know the Lord and *"walk in a manner worthy of the Lord, fully pleasing to him."* There are many other aspects of that which we have covered in the previous chapters.

Now I want to continue and show you that to live and grow in Christ in a hostile world we must recognize that Christ is first in everything. Let's look at Colossians chapter 1 verse 15: *"He* [God's beloved Son, verse 13] *is the image of the invisible God, the firstborn over all creation."* **Christ is the visible image of an invisible God.** *"God is Spirit"* we are told in John 4:24, and since God is spirit we cannot see him, we cannot touch him. How do we get to know God? He knew that was a problem, so God revealed Himself. God had to let people know He existed and what kind of a person He was. So how did He do it? In Old Testament times He sent his message through prophets—He met Moses on the mount, He revealed himself in special ways to His chosen people. But God in His great program went a step further than that. He decided the best way people would know Him was if He had a son and if He lived a human existence on earth.

Notice this actual statement of Jesus, John 14:9-11, where he told us one of the overwhelming purposes of his coming. Talking to Philip, one of his immediate disciples, he said: *"Have I been with you so long a time, and you still do not know me, Philip? Whoever*

43

has seen me has seen the Father. How can you say, 'Show us the Father'? [10]*Do you not believe that I am in the Father and the Father is in me? The words that I say to you I do not speak on my own authority, but the Father who dwells in me does his works.* [11]*Believe me that I am in the Father and the Father is in me, or else believe because of the works themselves."* Strong words and a bold claim from Jesus—a claim which eventually took him to the cross, because the religious leaders could not accept that Jesus declared himself to be the son of God and that if people would look at him they would see what God was like. You can imagine the reaction of the media today if I went on television and I said, "I am Christ, and if you look at me you'll see what God is like." I can just see the headlines tomorrow. In fact, I could see myself taken away by men in white coats to a mental institution. Yet that is what Jesus said. And so the question comes, Who is this Jesus? Who is this one who declared he was just like the Father. He went to the cross and died. He rose again from the dead. Who is he?

Every book of the Bible tells us something about this Jesus. If you want to know who he is, read the Book—it's even better than the film! Let's look at the wider context, since Colossians 1:15 starts with the pronoun "He". Backtrack to verses 13 and 14, where it teaches, *"Who has rescued us out from the authority of darkness and transferred us into the kingdom of his beloved Son,* [14]*in whom we have redemption, the forgiveness of sins."* First, this Christ Jesus who is first in everything, is our Savior. God is the one who rescued us from the domain of darkness. He is the one who removed us, took us from one place and put us in another. He moved us out of the influence of the negativity of sin and sickness, and He placed us in the kingdom of his Son, *"in whom we have redemption."* He released us from the power and penalty of sin. Not only are we released from having to pay for our sin, because he paid it, but we are released from the power of sin, the sin principle over our lives.

This Christ Jesus that we worship is our Savior, and I believe it is impossible to live God's way until you come to accept Christ as Savior. That's why we must reach people with this positive message. We're not telling them what miserable sinners they are and that they are going to Hell, as most of them already know that. We're telling them that God is love, that God has only the best for them—health, wealth, and happiness—and that they need to make that great affirmation that Jesus is Lord and Savior of their lives.

On to verse 15, and we read, *"He is the image of the invisible God"* The word "image" means an exact likeness, an accurate and perfect representation. I bear the family image of the Wades, and I have looked at the commonality in photos of my father in his early years and photos of myself at a similar age. People say, "He's the spitting image of his dad," "He's a chip off the old block." Now, certainly I have a similiar physical appearance as my father had in his early years, but I am not the exact likeness of my father because we have differences. We have differences in our personalities, we have differences in receding hairlines, and in other ways. I am not the exact likeness of my father, but I do bear a striking resemblance to him. However, the Word here in Colossians says that Jesus is the exact image of the Father.

So that's why it is important for people to understand Christ. The reason he came to earth was so that people could see that image. If that's what God is like, then I want to know everything there is about this God and I want to have a relationship with him. What did Jesus do? *"He went about doing good and healing all who were oppressed by the devil, for God was with him"* (Acts 10:38). He found a need and filled it. He found a hurt and healed it. If that is what Jesus did, then that is what God still wants to do today. *"He is the exact image of the invisible God, the firstborn over all creation"* (verse 15).

8

Everything is for Christ

Colossians 1:16-20

In verse 16 of Colossians one we come to another truth we need to learn about this person. *Christ Jesus is the ultimate purpose of creation.* The text does not say, "For by him were all things created" as we have in the King James and other versions. The word "by" in verse 16 is "in", see the Amplified Bible, American Standard Version, Weymouth, Young's, and others. *"For in him all things were created, in heaven and on earth, visible and invisible, whether thrones or dominions or rulers or authorities—all things were created through him and for him."* This verse is teaching against a heresy of the time that Christ was just one of many creatures that emanated from God, and that he himself was created. Notice the "for him" at the end of the verse. Christ is first in everything. Christ is the only way to God. Christ, in his relation to creation, has the same relationship as the Father. Christ was not created—he was born, and that is very different. He is the ultimate purpose of creation. And because we are in him then that makes mankind the reason for the heavens and the earth. Yet he is the ultimate purpose. Christ is first in everything.

47

Man lives to serve God/Christ

This beautiful universe around us and including us is for the ultimate purpose of Christ. It was created in his sphere of influence. It was created through him. It was created for him. One other point is that it says in verse 17, *"And he is before all things, and in him all things are held together"*. He is before all things. That is, he always comes first, and by him all things consist or cohere, are held together. All matter is made up of atoms and those atoms are chasing each other around endlessly and between them is a lot of space. What holds it all together? What keeps these tiny atoms in orbit? Christ! He is "the controlling and unifying force in nature" (Robertson). That's why Christ is important, because he's keeping this whole universe going.

Finally, it says verse 18, *"And he is the head of the body, the church. He is the beginning, the firstborn from the dead, that in everything he might be preeminent."* **Christ is the head of the body, the church.** Now that's a surprise to some people. They thought their pastor or the bishop was the head of the church. These people may be God's appointed leader in their local or regional situation, but Christ is the head of the church. If you lose sight of that fact, you have lost the ball game. We have to take our instructions, our guidance from Christ. If we fail to do that, then we will fail.

"He is the beginning, the firstborn from the dead." That is an interesting phrase, **the firstborn from the dead.** Birth and death seem to be two opposites, but Christ brought those opposites together in the resurrection, and he was the firstborn from the dead. This was so "that in everything he might be preeminent", the first. That is the critical thing. Many people do not deny that Jesus

walked this earth, they just demote him. They give him some prominence but they don't give him preeminence. We need to get back to seeing that the center of Christianity is Christ, and that the center of the Christian's life is the Christ that lives within us. All other things are peripheral to that fact. It is not about us, it's all about him. The central point is Christ.

"For in him all the fullness of God was pleased to dwell, [20]*and through him to reconcile to himself all things, through him, whether on earth or in heaven, making peace by the blood of his cross"* (verses 19-20). What does fullness mean here? "The totality of the Divine powers and attributes" (Lightfoot). The sum and total of all the divine attributes were wrapped up in a package and put within the victorious Christ Jesus. *"In him all the fullness of God was pleased to dwell"* and we'll learn more about that in Colossians chapter two. One other thing in verse 20, *"and through him to reconcile to himself all things." **Christ is the Reconciler.*** To reconcile is to bring back into harmony. This is not universal salvation. The ultimate aim of God is that the whole of nature around us, this whole universe, will come back in harmony with God. At the moment it is in disharmony.

At the fall of Adam and Eve all the thorns and briars were introduced to creation. They are all aberrations of a perfect creation. God's ultimate aim is to bring everything back into harmony with Himself, and He's going to do it through Christ. He will do it through the Reconciler, the one who brings things back together. The immediate work of Christ Jesus is to bring humanity back into harmony with God. We can be in harmony if we believe in Christ. II Corinthians 5:19 teaches us, *"In Christ God was reconciling the world to himself, not counting their transgressions against them, and entrusting to us the message of reconciliation."* When was God in Christ? When he was hanging on the cross; that was when God was reconciling the world to Himself.

So there are five things that the preeminent Christ is in this passage. He's our Savior. He's the Exact Image of God. He's the Ultimate Purpose of creation. He's the Head of the church. He is the Reconciler. Now, let's put this in practical terms. What is our response to this? It is simply this. We can acknowledge the truth but we must go further and acknowledge his authority as Lord over everything, including us. You see that in this passage. First, He is our Savior. He died on the cross, He rose from the dead. We have to accept that. By an act of our will we must say "I take that as my own history". We have to accept that He is the head of the church. We must make him first in everything. We must crown him Lord or Master of all.

"All" includes our homes, our business life. A friend of mine said to me that he keeps his religion and his business separate. That is impossible, because business is part of daily life. Business is a relationship between people. We call them companies because it is a company of people coming together for a common purpose to do a common thing. For a business to operate you are working with people. Christ must be crowned Lord of all in business as well. Are there any other areas? Marriage. We fail to recognize sometimes that after the wedding comes the marriage. It is like a violin. After the music has stopped the strings are still attached. If you're going to make a success of marriage you must crown him Lord of all in that situation as well. This is why I want you to see this truth as a basic to living a positive Christian life. He must be central in our everyday lives. Let us crown him as Lord of all in our lives and then let's enjoy living God's way in a hostile world.

9

Rags to Riches

Colossians 1:21-23

The first thing I noticed when I looked at this passage was that it is speaking directly to you and to me. Look how many times the word "you" appears. Verse 21, *"you, who once were..."* Verse 22, *"to present you."* Verse 23, *"the gospel that you heard."* Verse 24, *"my sufferings for you."* And then verse 26, *"now revealed to his saints"*—that's you and me, then verse 27 clearly says, *"Christ in you."* So this passage gets down to the specific, where you and I live.

First, in these verses we have a rags-to-riches story. It says in verse 21 that *"you, who once were alienated and enemies in your mind, doing evil deeds..."* In other words, we had turned our back on God and deliberately walked in the other direction. The word "alienated" refers to an estrangement. There was a feeling of hostility between us and God. It wasn't on God's side of the relationship—it was on our side. That feeling of hostility meant that we acted as the enemy. The strength of the Greek word is not just an enemy but an active, aggressive enemy. That was what we were. "We have met the enemy and he is us!" (Walt Kelly). Thank God we're not still there. The location of the problem people have with God is always in the mind. They think that God is against them and God always gets the blame for anything wrong that happens. People immediately say, "Why did God let this happen? Why did God make that person sick? Why did God kill that little baby?" God always gets the blame, and yet the problem is in people's minds. The hostility, the alienation against God is in the mind.

There are a number of verses I could quote on this point. Let me just quote Romans 5:8, *"But God shows his love for us, in that while we were still sinners, Christ died for us."* And then verse 10a says, *"For when we were enemies, we were reconciled to God by the death of his Son."* So even when we were in that state of being enemies, God still loved us, God still wanted the best for us. It was our stubborn mind, the six inches or 15 centimeters from ear to ear, that caused the hostility. We were enemies in our minds from God. That's the past and I thank God it's the past, don't you?

Let's look at the present then. We read in Romans 5:10 that while we were in that condition, *"we were reconciled to God by the death of his Son."* So we owe our present to the work of Jesus upon the cross. It's because he went to the cross that we have hope in the present. *"... Much more, being reconciled, we shall be saved by his life"* (verse 10b). Even more than that, *"we also rejoice in God through our Lord Jesus Christ, through whom we have now received the reconciliation"* (verse 11).

Now you can see the similarity of those statements as Colossians continues, *"... yet now he has reconciled [you] 23in his body of flesh by death, to present you holy, and blameless, and above reproach before him—"* (1:22-23a). Christ has presented us "holy, and blameless, and above reproach" before God. To be holy is to be separated unto God from evil. He wants us separated from that old life. To be blameless is to be without spot, without blemish. And to be above reproach means others are unable to pick any flaws in us, as ones who give no occasion for being brought before a court of law. We are free from accusation, because Jesus removed it on the cross. It does not happen because we do something now. The only thing we have to do now is to believe it.

It's not the way we live that makes us holy. It's because Jesus, the holy one, died in our place on the cross. So now because we have believed it, in God's sight we are holy. In God's sight we are flawless. In God's sight we are free from accusation. God's penetrating gaze, looking right down to the most minute thing in our lives, can only see in the present a holy, flawless, free child of God.

So folk, if God can see that, shouldn't we see it too? Can you see the problem that people have when they go through life thinking what miserable, wicked sinners they are? Thinking that they are just human and will never get it right? God has already got it right for you. He's just waiting for you to catch up with the information. If you believed and accepted God's gift of eternal life, in Christ you have a good standing.

God looks at you and sees a perfect, unique person! As far as you are concerned, you had better start thinking that same way too. Unless you have a healthy self-image of who you really are, you are not going to get far in this life. You are not going to live a positive Christian life thinking you are just a sinner saved by grace. It's very important to see this, for this is how God sees us— holy, flawless, free from accusation in His sight.

"Since indeed you continue in the faith, grounded and stead-fast, and are not drifting away from the expectation of the gospel

54

that you heard, which is being proclaimed in all the creation under heaven..." (Colossians 1:23). The word "if" can be translated "since." It's not "if" because it may not be so, but it is "since" for the sake of argument (see CLV, Companion Bible "assumed as an actual fact"). Let's continue on to the future, for while we have a tremendous present, we have a far more glorious future. That's why it's good to get up on Monday morning, because the future is right there. It has arrived at your doorstep. And we have an expectation. The word "hope" (KJV) should always be translated "expectation". We have a tremendous expectation for the future, because it is the expectation of the gospel. The good news of what God has done for you and what God sees you as being, and the power that God has resident within you—that good news is our expectation of the future, which we have heard and which is being proclaimed in all creation.

Our past is something that we don't want to think about. Most people have memories that bless and some memories that burn. God is not concerned with the past. I don't care where you come from but I am concerned as to where you're going—that is what my ministry is all about. The present is that we accept Christ Jesus as Lord and Savior. And in that acceptance we get a right standing with God. And the future? Well, "the future is as bright as the promises of God" (attributed to several classic preachers). "The future's so bright I gotta wear shades" (Pat MacDonald). That's the future that we have and I'm excited about that. So there is our past, our present, and our future.

Then verse 23b says, *"the gospel... and of which I, Paul, became a minister."* That's interesting, because a minister is not one who graduates from Bible College or Seminary. A minister is not one who is ordained. I don't know if you realize that. A minister is a person to whom God has given a ministry. I can go through Bible College or Seminary, get the parchment on the wall like I have, but did that make me a minister? No. That just said I completed a course of study. Let me apply it in another field. Just because you do a course of auto mechanics at a college, does that make you a mechanic? No. Studying all about it doesn't make you a mechanic. Something else is involved, like getting the car to run! And studying about the ministry doesn't make you a minister. It is God who gives a person the ability to become His minister. I think we should always recognize that. I'm not decrying the need for study. I would like to see every person in the church studying the word of God and finding out more about God. But that will not make every person in the church a minister. "A missionary is not a person who goes across the seas. A missionary is a person who sees the cross!" (J. Jay). Say that aloud until you get the point.

Paul was made a minister. A most unlikely choice, you must admit. Here was a man who went about killing Christians, and God turns him right around and he makes him a Christian instead. Quite a change! *"I, Paul, became a minister. 24Now I rejoice in my sufferings for you"* (verses 23b-24a). Remember, Colossians was written from jail. *"... And in my flesh I am filling up what is lacking in Christ's afflictions for his body, which is the church, 25of which I became a minister according to the stewardship from God which was given to me for you, to make the word of God fully known"* (verse 24b-25). *"I became a minister"*—twice he tells us that.

"According to the stewardship" or "administration" is how

I like to see it translated. The word is "a house economy", that is, a house steward or administrator. An administration is the way God is dealing with people at a particular period of time. This administration of God *was given to me for you, to make the word of God fully known."* There's "you" again. Whatever God tells me as a minister about the Word of God is not so I fill up my head with knowledge. He teaches it to me for you. That's how it works. And I get excited! God shares a lot of things with me that I have yet to share with you. The day will come. What I share with you is what God has given to me—that's the purpose of a ministry. It's a support situation and it is there to support the believers.

Now, of course, if you don't listen to the teaching then I can't minister to you, and what God has given to me won't help you one little bit. But I believe that I'm here because God shares things with me about the positive Word of God and I just can't wait for an opportunity to share them with you. That's how the process works. You get blessed by it. You may even pass it on to somebody else, and you should. There will be one thing which you probably pick up from this teaching that will inspire and excite you, and you should share that with somebody. Share it before the day is out, before you forget about it. Sharing will strengthen it in you and bless somebody else in the bargain.

So that's how the administration of God which is given to me for you works—to fulfill or to fully proclaim the Word of God, to fully discharge my office, the administration that God has given to me. It does not mean to complete the word of God, as one pastor tried to tell me recently. Paul didn't complete the Word of God, because other people wrote books after Paul had finished his

57

life—such as John, for example. The context is to fully proclaim the word of God, or to proclaim the full word of God to you.

10

The Great Mystery: Christ In You

Colossians 1:26-27

Now we come to the most exciting part of Colossians chapter one —verses 26 to 27. This is a very powerful section because it concerns a mystery. Let's talk about a mystery first before we get into this. My computer is a mystery. I can't understand how those "chips" do everything that I can see happening on the screen. But they do. They figure things out among themselves somehow. It's a mystery. I could go to college and learn exactly why and how. I do know enough about it now to realize how dumb that computer really is. Each "bit" in the memory has only two positions: on and off. That's right! My computer has millions of these little on/off switches in it and by the manipulation of those switches it does all the miracles of accounting and letter writing and everything else. So to most people a computer is a mystery, but it is not impossible to know. It is only a mystery because you are not fully initiated into the workings of a computer. So a mystery is not some matter that no one will ever know—it is knowable if you fully study that subject.

Verse 26 speaks of *"the mystery which had been hidden for ages and generations but now revealed to his saints."* Some prefer to translate the Greek word *musterion* as "secret", but I prefer the transliteration, "mystery". So until a point of time in earth's history, this great mystery was concealed. It was hidden to all the people in the Old Testament. They did not know it. It was hidden to the people in Gospel times. They did not know it. I believe it was even hidden from Jesus in his earthly walk, for he never mentioned it. It was a mystery which was "hidden for ages and generations but now..." Does "now" include the moment when it was written? Does it include the moment now when you are reading Colossians? Yes, "now revealed to his saints." In Bible terms, a saint is a person who believes in Christ. All of you who believe in Christ are saints. This mystery, it says, is now revealed to you. That's what I'm excited about. That is an incredible thing. I can remember the time when I really grasped this truth and I understood what it was saying.

God wants you to know what is this mystery, which is... and here it is! It states in verse 27, *"To whom* [his saints] *God willed to make known what are the riches of the glory of this mystery among the Gentiles, which is Christ in you, the expectation of glory."* The mystery is "Christ in you." Think about that! It is not "Christ among you," the church to whom this was originally written, but "the personal experience and presence of Christ in the individual life of all believers" *(Robertson's Word Pictures)*. Since Christ is in you, then you have a good help at hand. That's tremendous, folk.

Let's take the computer illustration again. I've now had a computer in my office for over a quarter of a century and had a website online since 1995. I'm starting to appreciate far greater what is in that box, but I'm not yet at the stage where I feel comfortable about it. And it's the same with this mystery in

Colossians. The moment you become a Christian, Christ comes within you, but you may not recognize He is there as you go on learning "what are the riches of the glory of this mystery". Now, hold that thought for a minute! Who has the best contact with God? Christ. And where is Christ? In you. Now that's something, isn't it? So it is not a case of whether God is going to deal with Peter Wade if he lives like Paul did. It has everything to do with the fact that God is in contact with the Christ that is in Peter Wade. The only thing that matters is that Peter Wade has Christ in him.

Colossians is teaching that all of Christ is in me, I'm "wall-to-wall" Christ. Every part of me should be a reflection of the Christ that is within. That is the mystery, the secret. I want to tell you something and it's a shame to have to say it, but there are a lot of Christians in your town or city who do not yet appreciate that Christ is in them. They know they are saved. They know they're going to heaven, but they have not yet tapped into the powerful truth of Christ in them. On Monday morning they may go to work, but it's actually Christ in them going to work. Think about that. What difference does that make to the job? A lot if you'll apply it. Who has a better connection to God than the Christ in you? No one! That's why I believe you have everything you need for every situation you will ever run across. And you have it not because you're smart or good looking, but because you have Christ in you, the expectation of glory. That is just part of the riches of the glory of this mystery.

Let's look at another part. Who better to meet the needs of humanity than that same Christ that is within? So when you run across people who are in need, it is not a question of whether you have the ability or the training to help that person meet their need. The question is, are you relying on and expressing the Christ within? Christ can meet the need. What did Jesus do when he was on earth? *"He went about doing good, and healing all who were oppressed by the devil, for God was with him"* (Act 10:38). If Christ went about doing good and we have Christ within us, then we can do that good also and help meet the needs of humanity. I like Annie Johnston Flint's poem that starts, "Christ has no hands but our hands to do his work today; He has no feet but our feet to lead men in the way." It is a beautiful poem. And as the oft-quoted saying encourages us, "Bloom where you are planted." The reason God has planted you where you are is because there are people with whom you rub shoulders, people next door, people where you work, who have needs and the answer to their needs is in the Christ that is in you. If we can duplicate this in other people, then we will change our society and our world. I really believe that. That's why I'm excited.

I have a vision of a map, with little lights flashing all over my city and around the world—representing people who have Christ in them. That's the effect of Christ being everywhere. That's why Christ had to die and go to heaven, because if he had stayed on earth there would have only been one Christ. Yet now God has made Christ available to everybody who believes. All over the world there are little lights flashing at this very moment. "Christ in you" is everywhere.

Do you get the excitement of that? If I was a TV evangelist I'd be hollering and screaming and pulling my hair out just to get you to see it. "All preaching is yelling, all teaching is telling!" But

I'm not an evangelist, I'm a teacher, and I don't have that much hair to pull out anymore! It's a great truth—it is "Christ in you" who is our expectation of glory. In Colossians 2:3 it says concerning Christ, *"in whom are hidden all the treasures of wisdom and knowledge."* That's why you don't need to know everything, because Christ knows it all. And where is Christ? Christ is in you the expectation of glory.

11

Proclaiming Christ

Colossians 1:28-29; 2:1-3

"Whom [Christ] we proclaim, warning everyone and teaching everyone in all wisdom, that we may present everyone mature in Christ. ²⁹For this I toil, striving according to his energizing which energizes me with power" (verses 28-29). The "whom" or "Him" is strong and significant. Paul preached a Person, not a philosophy. We need more ministers who would follow in Paul's footsteps and proclaim "Christ in you," to the end result of bringing believers to maturity in Christ. Notice the juxtaposition of "Christ in" and "in Christ" in verses 27 and 28. The two truths are required for completeness. Without a real knowledge of "Christ in you", you will not become "mature in Christ." Paul toiled to present these truths wherever he went, and God energized him for the task with power, the dynamic strengthening we saw earlier in verse 11.

"For I want you to know how great a struggle I have concerning you and those in Laodicea, and for as many as have not seen my face in the flesh" (Colossians 2:1). The chapter break is in an unfortunate place, but we know it is a human addition. There are three groups of people here: the Colossian believers, the believers in the church in nearby Laodicea, and believers everywhere who have

not seen or heard Paul in person (and that includes you and me).
Even though he was a prisoner in Rome, Paul was still striving for
the believers as he wrote this letter.

"That their hearts may be comforted, being joined together in
love, unto all riches of the full assurance of understanding, to a full
knowledge of the mystery of God the Father, and the Christ, ³in
whom are hidden all the treasures of wisdom and knowledge"
(2:2-3). The comfort for the saints was the strength of the teaching
just presented, and which Paul knew was far superior to the error
with which they were being attacked. Maturity in Christ can
withstand anything brought against a believer. What a contrast
to the child-like believers of Ephesians 4:14 who were *"tossed to*
and fro and carried about with every wind of teaching by the
cunning and cleverness of humans who lie in wait to deceive."
Knowing Christ is in you and you are in Christ brings stability to
the Christian life.

These Colossians believers now were on their way to the
"riches of the full assurance" and a "full knowledge" of the great
mystery. "Full assurance" appears three times in the New Testament. Here in Colossians 2:2 a "full assurance of understanding";
in Hebrews 6:11 a "full assurance of expectation"; and in Hebrews
10:22 a "full assurance of faith". The latter reference is often
printed with the words and music of one of our most loved
hymns:

> Blessed assurance, Jesus is mine,
> O what a foretaste of glory divine!
> Heir of salvation, purchase of God,
> Born of His spirit, washed in His blood.

Perfect submission, all is at rest!
I in my Savior am happy and blessed,
Watching and waiting, looking above,
Filled with his goodness, lost in his love.

(Fanny J. Crosby, 1873).

12

Get Your Head Straight

Colossians 2:4-7

We're ready to move on to a second major division of the book of Colossians. This is what we've learned so far: First, you must *get the basics straight.* A Christian is a unique person and because you are unique then you have positive Christian goals. It's important that we keep these goals in our mind so that we can maximize everything that God has made available for us. In order to do that we must make Christ first in everything and that's a great key. It's always Christ first! Then finally we learned the great mystery—Christ in you, the expectation of glory. And because you have Christ in you then you have a great contact with God and you are able to meet your needs and the needs of those around you.

Now we move on to a new major section. *Get your head straight!* Some years ago on Australian television there was a series of advertisements about a brand of pantyhose. A young lady was walking along in a mini skirt and the joggers who glanced at her ran into the lake, a cyclist finished up hitting the back of a truck, and a motorist ran into a fire hydrant. Everybody had a problem because they were distracted by looking at this attractive young lady. You cannot live your life like that. Get your head straight!

There are three words that begin with the letter "B" in Colossians 2:4 down to verse 15. Let's find them. In verse 4 there is the word "beguile" (KJV, CLV). Beguile, that is a wonderful word. And then in verse 8 we have the word "beware" (KJV, NKJV, CLV, Moffatt). Do you see that? Beware! And finally in verse 14 we have these unusual words in the Bible, "blotting out" (KJV, ASV). I want to underline those three words, and use them as key words that we will follow. This section will require your careful reading, so you may want to read it in more than one sitting.

Beguile

Let's start at verse 4. *"And this I say lest anyone may beguile you with persuasive words."* What is the context? We are taught in verse 3 that in Christ *"are hid all the treasures of wisdom and knowledge".* *"And this I say lest any man should beguile you...."* Think about that word "beguile". What image does it bring up for you? Perhaps a glittering TV advertisement! Beguiling, deceiving, deluding—making it look attractive so it takes your attention off of one thing and gets you to put it on something else. In other words, it turns your head. It is trying to stop you keeping your head straight for the goal of maximizing all that God has made available to you. The word "beguile" means to lead astray by false reasoning, to cheat by false reckoning, to amuse or charm. It may look attractive but it is built upon a false foundation. So there's the battle, and the battle will always continue in the mind. We must take control of what we think about because what you think is what you say and what you say can work blunders as well as wonders.

Do not let *"anyone... beguile you with persuasive words"*—persuasive, deceitful, enticing words (the Greek word is only used here in the New Testament). I don't have to tell you that the battle today is for the minds of people. The media knows this. The advertising world knows this. The political parties know this. And the different ideologies and religions know this. The battle is to get the minds of people. That battle does not cease just because I became a Christian. The battle continues. In fact, if the truth is known, the battle gets stronger because there are people who want to "beguile me with persuasive words" and take me away from the foundation I have in Christ, who is the center of my life.

Verse 5 continues with the positive side of that statement. *"For though indeed I am absent in the flesh, yet I am with you in spirit."* Paul had never visited the church at Colossae. He had had no part in its foundation except that he shared the word of God with Epaphras and some of the citizens of Colossae who had gone to Ephesus to hear him speak, and they had gone back home and started a fellowship. Their response had impressed Paul, and he told them he was *"rejoicing to see your order and the steadfastness of your faith in Christ."*

"Order" is a word that relates to a **soldier**. It means to be in ranks, in line, and when facing the enemy there is no breach. One of the first things that new recruits learn in boot camp is how to stand in line, how to make up that rank. It is a word rarely used in the Bible. Paul is saying that Christians are like soldiers standing in ranks. Christians should see that to live God's way in a negative world it is necessary to have order, it is necessary to have discipline. It is self-discipline that gets you through. I cannot dictate from the pulpit or podium. I can only motivate you with the Word of God. Each one of us needs order in our lives. It is interesting here that this word "order" is used in relation to the attempt of people to beguile us with persuasive words. We must stand in rank—a sign that the soldier is ready for any command, just standing there at attention, in rank.

The next word, "steadfastness", is also a military term. One translation has it that you present a "solid front" (Moffatt), and it goes back to the days of battle when you had soldiers walking towards the enemy in an horizontal line as a solid front. That's the meaning of the word here—stability, firmness, strength. To have a solid front, to stand "shoulder to shoulder" (The Letters of Saint Paul, Arthur S. Way, 1901). So when we are beguiled with persuasive words, when somebody tries to turn our head away from the completeness that we have in Christ, let's stand in rank, take that solid front. Let's click our heels and let the world know that we cannot be moved because what we have is something far greater than what they have out there in the world. Do you believe that? So act like a soldier. That's the first picture here of the progress of the Christian from the moment they become a Christian until they learn to appreciate and appropriate God's power within us. The first picture is of a soldier standing firm in rank, in order, ready for anything that might happen. As the gospel song says, "I am His to command where He leads me" (Phil Kerr).

Paul continues in verse 6 with this powerful statement: "Therefore, as you received Christ Jesus the Lord, so walk in him." In the same manner as you received him, so walk in him. The word "received" is in the sense of learned. I should also note that "Christ Jesus the Lord" is not used anywhere else in Paul's epistles. "As you received Christ Jesus the Lord, so walk in him." "As... so..." So, how did you receive him? Romans 10:9 states that *"If you confess with your mouth that Jesus is Lord and believe in your heart that God raised him from the dead, you will be saved."* To walk in Bible terms refers to your manner of life, the way you conduct yourself. How then do we "walk", live the Christian life? By belief and by confession (affirmation).

This is a different picture from the previous verse. A soldier doesn't walk—a soldier marches. So the picture has changed to that of a **pilgrim** who is walking, searching for truth, always walking. So keep on walking (present active tense) in the same way as you received Christ. How are we to walk? We will live our lives as pilgrims, because that is what the Bible says we are. Our citizenship is in a heavenly country (Philippians 3:20) and here on earth we are just strangers, pilgrims. We are to walk in this life using our believing and making our affirmations. Walk, it says, in the same manner as you received him.

Notice the "in him" again. There's "faith in Christ" in verse 5, "walk in him" in verse 6, and "rooted and built up in him" in verse 7. So our walk is to be on the basis of our position, "in him." The potential for a lengthy and profitable study of what that means in the Pauline writings can be seen from that statement.

"Having been rooted" (verse 7). What does it mean to be "rooted" (only here and Ephesians 3:17)? Once again the picture changes. Now it is a natural picture, in particular a **growing tree**. It's interesting because the tense changes here to "having been rooted once and forever." This is the crisis experience which we call salvation; it is both a fact and a truth. It happened and nothing is going to change it. It is established and secure. Our

71

roots are down deep in Christ, to use the picture. Now we know what is holding us in place. Our roots are "in him."

Yet the next phrase, *"built up in him,"* is in the continuous tense. So we can translate it *"having been rooted and being built up in him."* The building is progressing, it is still under construction. Now we have an architectural picture. How is your **building** progressing? You see, what Christ placed within me when I received him is perfect, permanent, and has potential. That's solid truth—that's everything that Christ is in me, my foundation. But the appreciation of it, the awareness of it, the understanding of it is here in my mind. How are we *"being built up in him"*? By reading his Word, by taking in the concepts that he has made available for us, by talking to Him and developing the relationship.

So we've gone from a military world to the pilgrim world, to the natural world, and now the architectural world. They are all pictures of our growth as positive Christians. And it doesn't stop there. It continues, *"and established in the faith, just as you were taught."* Now we are in **school**. I've often said that the best model of the church universal is as an educational institution. We are here to teach people. We are not a first-aid station to place a Band-Aid on a situation. We are not a country club, for people to come and relax and feel good about themselves once a week.

Do you know the old Chinese proverb, "Give a man a fish and he'll eat for a day; teach him how to fish and he'll eat for a lifetime"? To give him the fish is a Band-Aid. Yes, there are times for that kind of situation. But the lasting work that the church does is as a teaching institution. It says here in verse 7 that we are

GET YOUR HEAD STRAIGHT

"established in the faith, just as you were taught." "Established" is
to be made firm and stable, and teaching establishes us. That's
why we need to listen to positive teaching. That's why we need to
use our time in the car to listen to audio teachings. We need also
to read and listen to what God says in the Bible every day, because
a verse a day keeps the devil away. We need all those inputs to
teach us, to establish ourselves in the faith. I'm tired of being
yelled at when I watch Christian television or go to church. We
need good teaching, for it establishes us, helps us progress in our
faith journey.

And finally verse 7 says *"overflowing in it in thanksgiving."*
The overflowing ("abounding" KJV) is like a *river* that cannot
contain the volume of water flowing in it. Overflowing with
thanksgiving. Not just saying "Thank you" when we slip into bed
at night or just saying "Thank God that day is over" or even saying
"Well, thank you Lord, that was exciting. I wonder whether we can
top it tomorrow." Not just saying thank you but overflowing with
thanksgiving. So now the picture is aquatic, of water. It is
interesting the way in which all these illustrations are given. Each
one is trying to get one part of the truth across to us in terms we
can understand.

So we have seen the ways we should handle those people
who want to beguile us, those people who want to entice us with
nice-sounding phrases (verse 4). We keep our head straight and
first recognize that we have been rooted and can and must progress in the faith. Verses 4-7 are key verses to a positive, practical
Christian life in a hostile world.

73

13

God Says "Beware"

Colossians 2:8-10

We are now ready for chapter 2 verse 8. As I walk around our district a lot, I see many gates with a sign on them: "Beware of the dog." Sometimes I wonder if they have just put the sign on the gate or whether there is really a dog on the property. In addition, many security-conscious people get hold of stickers that say that "This place is being watched by..." whoever, even if it isn't. Or "These premises are under electronic surveillance," even though it is not. All these signs are trying to discourage people from entering the property.

However, I want to tell you something. When God says "Beware," He means what He says! God has looked down the corridors of time and he sees that you need to be warned of certain things. When God says "Beware," sit up and take notice! We need to learn what God wants us to watch out for. So this is the second B in Colossians chapter 2. The word "beware" here means to look out for something, to take heed to what you have been told. Keep your eyes open. Stay alive. Stay alert. Why? Because there are situations happening around you and if you go to sleep on the job then life could become difficult.

What does it say we are to beware of? *"Beware that no one takes you captive through philosophy and vain deceit, according to the tradition of men, according to the elements of the world, and not according to Christ"* (verse 8). To take captive ("spoil", KJV) means to plunder or rob, to carry you off as bounty. In the old days, when one nation invaded another nation, they would take all the treasures and many of the people back home with them as slaves. Don't let anyone take away your faith as a bounty. Don't let them control you with "so-called philosophy and intellectualism and vain deceit (idle fancies and plain nonsense)" (Amplified).

Now it does not mean that all philosophy is wrong. Philosophy is the love and pursuit of wisdom, and we need wisdom if we are going to make it through this life positively and successfully. God is not against all philosophy but He is talking about a vain and deceitful philosophy. The word "vain" means useless as to its effect, actually "empty", and "deceit" means it is going to lead us astray. Through what ways is this so-called philosophy going to affect us? It will be through reliance on human tradition and the elements of this world. There's one problem—human tradition. Now some traditions are good. I'm traditional. I always like to meet with my family at Christmas time and celebrate family birthdays—they are good traditions.

Yet there are some traditions that we need to re-examine in the light of the Word of God. Traditions can be good, and traditions can be limiting and even harmful. We need to examine them all. The kind of traditions mentioned here are obviously those which are holding people back from maximizing all that they can be. Then there are the elementary principles of the world. The "old wives' tales" of the world: rites, rules, regulations. Some are true but many are in error. And *not according to Christ*—there's the real problem, they are not the principles that Christ teaches. We do not measure Christ by the philosophies, we must measure the philosophies by Christ.

If we follow the Christ pattern for successful positive living, we're going to have a great life. The problem with these other things is that they turn our heads away from Christ to something else, and we're in trouble already. We've allowed our attention to be taken off the One who has the guidance we need. If I stay my attention on Christ, if I put Christ first in everything, then I have total supply—happiness, health, and wealth. That's a guarantee that we all ought to be thankful for. So God says "beware," because there are people trying to turn your heads and get you looking in another direction, but if you do, you'll miss out. Beware, there's danger ahead! So what is our defence?

"For in him [Christ, previous verse] *the whole fullness of deity dwells bodily"* (verse 9). This is an incredible verse. In Christ dwells all the fullness, the sum and total of all the attributes and character of God. The Greek word for "deity", *theotes*, occurs nowhere else in the New Testament. Yet verse 10 is even more mind-boggling. It says, *"And you are complete in him"* (KJV), literally "you are in Him filled full." Christ has the sum total of the divine and you are totally *complete* in Him. This is the first of a five-fold identification with Christ, our defence against the dangerous philosophies. Think about that word "complete". I studied the Syriac (Aramaic) language for a while, in which many people believe the New Testament was originally written. It has

76

Happiness / Health / Wealth

an intensive form of the verb that could be rendered "you are totally complete in Him" or "you are completely, completely, complete in Him." Think about it. Was Christ ever sick? No. Was Christ ever poor? No. Did Christ get on with people? Yes He did.

You have Christ in you. You are complete in Him. That's the power of the Christian. That's why it pays to stay alert. That's why it pays to take notice of the "beguile" (verse 4) and the "beware" (verse 8). Read through the gospels and the book of Acts. Find out what Jesus was really like. And that Jesus is the Christ Who is within you. He is the victorious One within you. And you are complete in Him. Now, that is powerful. Verse 10 concludes, *"who* [Christ] *is the head of all rule and power."* He alone is God's underruler, the firstborn among many brethren (Romans 8:29), *"the firstborn from the dead; that in all things he might have the preeminence"* (Colossians 1:18). And you are complete in Him.

14

You are Identified with Christ

Colossians 2:11-15

Not only are you "complete in Him" (verse 10), but there's more! The "in whom" [Christ] at the start of verse 11 introduces this section down to verse 15. All you are about to read relates to past events and you participated in those events because of your identification in Christ. *"In him also you were circumcised with a circumcision made without hands, in the putting off of the body of the flesh in the circumcision of Christ"* (verse 11). **Circumcision** is to cut off part of the human flesh, and what God has cut off in our personal life is the power and penalty of sin. This "putting off" is likened to not only removing a garment from the body but disposing of the garment as well. The flesh is no longer under the dominion of sin... that is a great truth to know. And verse 12 teaches *"having been buried together with him in baptism, in which you were also raised together through the faith of the operation of God, who raised him from the dead."* The Greek tense indicates all three events happened at the same time: circumcised, buried, raised.

We are **buried** with Him in His baptism. We were identified with him in this action. It's not talking about water here. It refers to His baptism into death. We were buried with him in His baptism. And then we were **raised** with him through the operation of God's faith at the resurrection of Jesus from the dead. There is a further step upwards in verse 13. *"And you, who were dead in your trespasses and the uncircumcision of your flesh, He made alive together with him, having forgiven us all our trespasses."* We have been quickened (KJV) or **made alive** together with him. "Made alive"—God made you *"dead to sin but alive to God in Christ Jesus"* (Romans 6:11). Circumcised, buried, raised, made alive, forgiven—these all became ours in an instant when we accepted Jesus as Lord of our life.

God does not look at our past but He looks at Christ, because "His story" has become our "history." We are identified with Christ in all He did for humanity. When He was crucified, we were crucified. When He died, we died with him. When He was buried, we were buried with Him. Yet, praise God, when He was raised, we were raised with him. When He was made alive, we were made alive with him!

Ephesians 2:6 takes it one step further when it teaches that God *"raised us up with him and seated us with him in heavenly places in Christ Jesus."* When Christ sat on the right hand of God, in God's sight we too are **seated** together with Him. So the list goes on... raised, made alive, forgiven, given seating! The throne life is what it is all about. The Father has greater purposes in mind than our limited time on this earth, so He gives us a foretaste by opening the curtains of heaven and showing us how He sees us! In His eyes we are already in the throne room of heaven! I want to tell you, folk, we are powerful Christian people, and God wants us to expand our awareness of it and use His power for His glory.

[See my teaching article "Identified with Him" in both English and Spanish on our web site, www.peterwade.com.]

Blotting out

Now we come to verse 14 and our third "B" word. *"Having blotted out the handwriting of ordinances that was against us, which was contrary to us, and took it out of the midst, nailing it to the cross."* What was on the indictment, the charge sheet, against us? It was the record of our sin, as we know from the last part of verse 13, *"having forgiven us all our trespasses."* So we are free from the power and penalty of sin, and free from our past. The "blotting out" is a reality.

In the early years of my life, you could call up a collection agency and say, "What do you know about the ABC Printing Company?" And they would tell you that they pay their bills on time, where they banked, and so on. In Bible days they didn't have that sort of setup. I am thankful to Bishop K.C. Pillai for teaching me the Eastern custom, since the Bible is an oriental book. If a person had some debts they would make out a list and would write, "Here are the debts of Peter Wade. He owes X amount to this person, so much to this person..." and so on. The debtor would have to sign at the bottom. Then they would take that notice to the elders of the gate and they would post it at the gates of the town, on the bulletin board as it were. If you wanted to know whether Peter Wade was a good credit risk, you'd check the bulletin board first and see if he gets a mention. This was the custom of the day. It must have been the ultimate embarrassment!

Often that person had no way of paying off his debts. He needed someone else to come to his help. So Peter Wade would go to talk to his rich uncle and say, "Uncle, I need some help. Would you please come and pay off my debts, and I'll do this and that for you?" So the uncle would pay off those debts one by one. Then he would go to the elders of the gate and inform them that all Peter Wade's debts have been paid. The elders would go to that sheet of debts pinned at the gates, and they would fold it double, fold it in half so the back of the sheet was all you could see—a clean sheet—and nail it back on the "bulletin board." From that moment, Peter Wade can walk around the town knowing that his debts are paid and his credit rating is good once again. That is what it is talking about here in verse 14. "Cancelled", "wiped out", "erased", other translations say. *"The slate wiped clean, that old arrest warrant cancelled and nailed to Christ's Cross"* (Message Bible). God doubled it over as it were, and nailed it to the cross.

Another example of this Orientalism is found in Isaiah 40:2. It says, *"Speak comfort to Jerusalem, and cry out to her, that her warfare is ended, that her iniquity is pardoned; For she has received from the Lord's hand double for all her sins"* (NKJV). If her iniquity is pardoned, she cannot receive double for them! Is it a problem with the translation? No, it is an Orientalism, the custom that I have just described for you. The list of her sins has been doubled over and they are no longer charged against her anymore. That's the concept of that beautiful passage. And that is what happened for you and for me. Jesus Christ has paid for our sins. God has blotted out the handwriting that was against us. *"And having disarmed principalities and powers, He made a show of them openly, triumphing over them in it* [or in himself]" (verse 15). He made a show, an example of our enemies; He put them on display for the whole universe to see. Christ was the victor and we have our victory in him.

15

Let No One Judge You

Colossians 2:16-17

To get our heads straight we need to continue on in Colossians chapter 2. There are some very powerful statements here about things we need to know and do if we are going to live and grow in Christ in a hostile world. We are in that area where the believer needs to beware of "isms". It is difficult when the "isms" try to label us and make us something that God does not plan us to be.

Now as I share these truths with you, I do recognize the fact that it is important that we respect every person's right to practice their religion in the way they want. That is an important point, but even more important we must recognize that we need to take our Christianity from the Christ of the Bible and not from other people. That is a vital distinction. We do not take our Christianity from what other people do, however spiritual they may seem to be. We only take it from the Christ of the New Testament, and in particular I should point out we need to take it from the risen Christ of the church epistles, not the Jesus of the beard and the sandals. We must follow the risen Christ, the Lord Jesus Christ. *"God has made this same Jesus, whom you crucified, both Lord and Christ"* (Acts 2:36). Now in order for me to illustrate the truths in this and the following chapters I will mention certain religious practices that are observable in my fair city and yours also, and I do so merely to illustrate and not to condemn, because I think I need to make the truth clear.

So let's go to verse 16. *"Therefore let no one judge you in food, or in drink, or in respect of a holy day, or of the new moon, or of the sabbaths."* The first word in many translations is "Therefore" (ESV, NASB, AMP, etc.), a connecting word. So what we are about to discover is firmly based on the prior section (verses 4-15), which we looked at in the previous chapters under the key words "Beguile," "Beware," "Blotting out," and particularly the latter. God in Christ made you alive, having forgiven you all your trespasses, and triumphed publicly over your enemies.

It's time to note the key word, and it is a verb, as it so often is. I have it underlined in my Bible, and this is the simple little word "let." Let no one judge you. The problem here is **legalism**. Whenever the Bible says "let" it is saying the subject is something you have control over. It's your life. You are in charge and it's up to you if you allow other people to judge you or not. I do not allow it in my life. I respect other people's opinions but I will take no notice of their judgments. Let no one judge you. It tells us in this verse about some things that those criticizing the Colossians were very clever in judging people: in food or drink, and in respect of a holy day, the new moon, and sabbaths. To judge of course means to pronounce a sentence, to come out with a critical judgment about you.

First, no one should judge us about eating or drinking. Diet seems to be an important concept of some people's lives. I may not have a great problem in that area, although I am careful what I eat. But other people seem to make dieting the pride of life and that's their privilege and maybe their necessity! However, we're talking here about those people who say we shouldn't eat or drink certain things because of religious motives. For example, there are some groups who would say that you should not drink tea or coffee or Coca-Cola. Why do they say that? Well, they feel these are harmful to the body, but the problem comes when those people say if you do drink them then you are not the spiritual kind of person that God wants you to be. Now, folk, that becomes a real challenge.

Diet is one thing. Dress is another. Some people say that we should dress in a certain way. When we lived in the Midwest of America we often ran across the Amish people in Ohio and Pennsylvania. They dress as their ancestors did in the 1800s. Women wear long black dresses and the men suits with wide brimmed hats, and so on. They ride in their horse-drawn carts. They do not believe that any of the modern inventions like cars and telephones and television are blessed of God. So there are many people who would criticize on dress. I don't believe in those restrictions. How you dress does not make you a better or a worse Christian. There are moral standards to be maintained of course but it's not a question of your spirituality that is at stake.

Then there are others who would judge people according to the days in which they do certain things. I was brought up in an era when it was considered wrong to do certain household tasks on a Sunday. We would never have the copper boiling clothes on a Sunday (before washing machines). That was just taboo. Nor would we use the wringer (before dryers) or the iron. On a Sunday women would never get the sewing machine out. In fact, in my childhood I can recall that my mother would never cook a meal on a Sunday. The day had some great importance to my parents. So there are some of the restrictions that people would tend to put upon us. Some groups substitute Saturday for Sunday, but the problem is the same.

So what does verse 16 say? *"Therefore let no one judge you"* in respect of these things. You can live a very happy, positive, fulfilled life so long as you don't allow their judgment or their condemnation of your actions to get to you. You won't stop them judging you, that is true. But you are in total control of your reaction to what they are saying. And if you react to them in a negative way, then you're the one who has lost the peace and joy of living. They will just go on down the street and criticize someone else, because your reaction didn't affect them at all. So that is what Paul is getting at here. We want to enjoy the full Christian life, so let's beware of legalism, when people who want to label us for certain actions.

I've mentioned it before but it's a good illustration. One denomination of which I was a member in the 1950s had a Church Manual, and in this manual it listed a number of things that members should not do. One was that I should not read the Sunday newspaper, or rather the newspaper on Sunday. Also I should not go to circuses, theaters or like places of public entertainment. I should not engage in mixed bathing, and so it went on. I have often told how I got around those restrictions, because *"The heart is deceitful above all things, and desperately wicked"* (Jeremiah 17:9). It just so happens in the downtown area of Adelaide at that time you could buy the Sunday newspaper on Saturday evening, which we did and read it on Saturday evening. So that took care of that legalism. It was not until our family moved to America to live that we understood this prohibition. The Sunday papers were as thick as a John Grisham novel, and would take all day to read! In the 2005-09 edition of that church's manual, there is no prohibition of Sunday newspapers, so perhaps we were not sinning in the 1950s after all! Nor is there now any mention of circuses, theaters, or mixed bathing.

At one time we had some folk in our fellowship who had belonged to a group where they were absolutely forbidden to have conversation or social contact with people who had not accepted Christ within the framework of that group. It was a very exclusive group. They believed only the people who were saved by listening to their preachers were the ones who were going to make it to heaven. Because of this they should be very careful about their contact with other people. These are very real things that are happening right in our city today. In fact, I conducted a wedding for one person who had some relatives in that particular group, and they did everything they could to avoid me on that wedding day because I represented the doubtful ones with whom they would not have to share heaven. Beware of "isms." In particular, beware of legalism.

"These are a shadow of the things to come, but the body [substance] *is of Christ"* (verse 17). Shadows, "a dim outline of future things, not the reality" (Albert Barnes). The reality only comes from Christ (the word "Christ" is used seven times in

Colossians chapter 2). The Christians who judge you on the five outward actions of verse 16 are chasing shadows and not Christ. By having Christ within us we have a solid foundation for positive Christian living, and all those other things are merely peripheral to that and are not going to count in the final analysis. As my good friend Norman Campbell says, it doesn't matter what tag you've got on—if you go up it's going to blow off and if you go down it will burn off, so all tags are meaningless! Denominations wrap around us as part of Christian worship rituals, rules, and regulations, but they are meaningless as far as God is concerned. So let no one judge you in legalism.

16

Let No One Beguile or Enslave You

Colossians 2:18-23

Then Paul continues in verse 18, *"Let no man beguile you of your reward"* (KJV). This is not the same word for "beguile" as we had in verse 4 of chapter 2 but it is a word that means let no one be an umpire in a contest to your detriment, that is, to disqualify you. *"Let no one disqualify you"* (ESV). I can relate to this very well. In my track career I competed in what was called race walking. There are certain rules in that race that have to be observed, and two are fundamental. One is that the feet must remain in contact with the ground at all times, and secondly that the supporting leg must straighten on contact with the ground and remain straight while the body passes over it. In order to make sure that athletes abide by these rules, there are four or more officials stationed around the track. Tests have proved that even using standard film or video cameras at 25-30 frames per second, it is not possible to judge whether a race walker has maintained contact with the ground. Only video taken with a slow-motion camera can detect this, so the controversy continues even at Olympic level. In my entire walking career only once did I get disqualified, and I was highly offended by this action. This is what Paul is writing about here. Let no one umpire you in a negative way.

And what is it concerning? *"...Taking delight in false humility and worship of angels, intruding into those things which he has not seen, in vain being puffed up by his fleshly mind"* (verse 18). The idea is that these false teachers "did not announce their opinions with dogmatic certainty, but they would put on the appearance of great modesty" (Barnes). The implication is that any truths thought to be received from these sources are simply what people have perceived in their minds. This is **mysticism**. What is the real problem? Verse 19, *"and not holding fast to the Head...."* The real problem is that they have deserted Christ as the Head. To them Christ is a great Teacher and Leader, but not our Lord and Savior. As a result they have no relationship with Christ.

We need to maintain a consciousness of being one with Christ, of being "in Christ" and Christ being "in us." Christ is the Head *"from whom all the body, nourished and knit together through its joints and ligaments, grows with the growth of God"* (verse 19b). The head controls the body. It is not the taste buds that control the body. The head sends signals back and forth to all the parts of the body. Our whole body is related to the head, and as Christians we too are related to the Head, who is Christ. As we keep that relationship and keep the consciousness, the awareness of that relationship, then all these other weird and wonderful things that people throw across our path will have no meaning. I believe it is Christ plus nothing, and I really mean that. It is Christ plus nothing that makes all the difference in life, in fact, that gives us our victory.

Let no one enslave you

Let's go on to the last part of chapter 2. We have seen "Let no one judge you," "Let no one beguile you," and now "Let no one enslave you." Verses 20-23 read, *"Since you died with Christ from the basic principles of the world, why, as living in the world, do you submit to ordinances: [21]'Do not handle, Do not taste, Do not touch', [22]which things perish as they are used, according to human commands and teachings? [23]These things indeed have a reputation of wisdom in inventing worship and mock humility and self-denial to the body* [asceticism], *but they are of no value against the indulgence of the flesh."*

Asceticism comes from the word used for a monk or a hermit, and refers to people who engage in self-denial in order to make some spiritual progress. Whether that means fasting during Lent in a ritualistic context or whether it means shutting yourself away from the world, wearing a rough, hairy robe and sleeping on a hard bed—it is denying yourself. *Asceticism* goes hand in hand with legalism... "Do not handle, Do not taste, Do not touch." There are a lot of people who still feel more comfortable in religious Christianity if they are told to do something. And they likewise feel comfortable if they are told to believe something. There is something within our inherent nature that we feel we must do something, especially when an authority figure is doing the telling. We're not happy just relaxing and being a living expression of Christ Jesus.

In verse 20 notice the passive nature—*"why... do you submit to ordinances?"* Why do you allow yourself to be subjected to people who say "Don't, don't, don't"? So can we still be in control of our lives?

Absolutely! You've got the "let" in verse 16, the "let" in verse 18, and now you have this statement in verse 20, "why... do you submit?" There is no reason for these regulations. They have "a reputation, an appearance of wisdom" but "they are of no value" (verse 23).

So if you still feel you have to take some step, some action in order to have full spiritual power or growth, then according to Paul you are being misled. The text says that these things all perish with the using and have been obtained from human teaching. They are all transient things. Christian television today is swamped with teachers telling you what you should or must do in order to have this or that or go to a higher level. It is mostly nonsense, human teaching of "no value." In the church age, it is not what you eat or drink or do that counts. What is important is what you have—Christ within! *"For* [in Christ Jesus] *neither circumcision and uncircumcision counts for anything; the only thing that matters is a new creation"* (Galatians 6:15 NET Bible).

Christ in you is permanent, so there's no reason to go down the road of self-disciplining the body to gain spiritual progress. Now, some of us are living evidence that a little self-discipline wouldn't hurt. I'm not talking about that! I'm talking about the fact of doing it to gain spiritual growth, doing it to make yourself a spiritually better person. It is not necessary. We have Christ within us, the expectation of glory.

I believe that the Christ within us is so perfect, so totally complete (verse 9) that we have no need for anything else. We do not have to add anything to it. We do not have to do anything about it. We merely have to believe it. That's the beautiful teaching of the New Testament as I read it. We are complete in Him.

Let's review all this. I have a chart that I picked up somewhere about verses 16-23 which says, "We don't grow by addition but by appropriation." That is a very good statement. There is legalism on the one side, pictured by the Mosiac tablets of stone. Then there is mysticism, beautifully pictured by a crystal ball. Next there is asceticism, with a picture of a shapely lady on the cross with a sheet of paper headed "Approved Diet"! And finally there is a book of "False Philosophies" of the world. All these are attempts to add something to the Christ within, and "they are of no value." On the other hand there are the things we appropriate by our faith in Christ, which things we have resident within. We tap into the spirit of life in Christ Jesus. We have freedom, stability, victory. We have grace, joy, and probably a hundred other things that could be listed.

We appropriate all our blessings. We don't have to add anything because our situation with our God is described very beautifully in the New Testament. In fact, it's in this same chapter. Verses 9 and 10 describe exactly how God sees me and how I am to see myself. "*For in him* [Christ, previous verse] *the whole fullness of deity dwells bodily; and you are complete in Him.*" Total completeness. Nothing can be added to it. If you are complete, then you are complete. If the chess board is complete, it's complete; you don't chase around and find another couple of pieces to put on the board.

Completeness, believer, is completeness. When God says we are complete, I believe it. I accept it. You have real confidence from knowing that the Christ within you is complete, and you are complete in Him.

17

Be Willing to be Different

Colossians 3:1-4

We are halfway through the book of Colossians. I think it's a good time to pause and see that chapters one and two had some solid teaching for us on how to live and grow in Christ in a hostile world. Chapters three and four are going to make that practical. There is often this balance in Paul's letters, because it is not enough to declare and defend the positive truth of God's Word—what we need are people who also demonstrate it. Ephesians is another of Paul's letters where we see this division; chapters one to three contain solid teaching on what Christ has done for us, while chapters four to six show us how to make that teaching practical. You can see this in other letters also.

As a teaching ministry, we could fill your minds with all kinds of wonderful positive knowledge from God's Word. We could lay out the principles one by one, but I believe our ministry would fail if we were not generating people who get out there and make it work. We need people who demonstrate the truth by making it happen in their everyday lives. So we have come to this most important part of the book of Colossians. This is where the rubber meets the road. This is what we have to do to live and grow in Christ.

I started by dividing the book into three parts and the first one of those was to *get the basics straight.* We saw that the Christian is a unique person, and you are unique because you are walking around with Christ in you, the expectation of glory. And then we moved on to seeing that we must have positive Christian goals. The number one goal in life is to put God first and to allow God's will and Word to direct our activities. Then we discovered that Christ is first in everything, and unless we put Him first in everything then we are less likely to ask for His help in our everyday life. Finally, we saw the truth that there was a great secret and that was "Christ in you, the expectation of glory."

The second part of our discussion concerned our need to *get our heads straight.* In Colossians 2 we found that not only are we alive but we have to stay alert. There are many people alive but some of them are asleep with their hands on the switch. The Bible says there are things of which we need to beware. There are people who are trying to drag us down, and we have to beware of the "isms." There was mysticism, asceticism, and legalism, to name a few "isms." Now we will see our need to *get our lives straight.*

Seek and set and source

We are ready for Colossians chapter three, verse one. *"Since then you have been raised with Christ, seek those things that are above, where Christ is, seated at the right hand of God."* Let me explain the first word, "if" (KJV and others). "The hypothesis is assumed as an actual fact" (Bullinger, Appendix 118, *Companion Bible*); it is only "if" in the sense of the argument. It is really saying "since" or "in view of the fact" that you have been risen with Christ. It is already an established situation. In view of that fact then you should "seek"—underline that word—"seek those things that are above." We learned in school that "seek" is a verb, a word of action. It's something you and I have to do. We are already risen with Christ from our old life to our new life. That happened for us when we became a Christian, yet Colossians is written to Christians and it is saying for us to "seek those things which are above." That means spiritual things. So even though you are a Christian, there is some effort necessary to live and grow in Christ in a hostile world. We must seek spiritual values.

Then in verse 2 we need to underline the word "set". So far there are two things we have to do: seek spiritual values and set something. *"Set your minds on things that are above, not on things that are on earth."* So that's how we seek spiritual values. We put the "upward things" (Greek text) in our minds. We set our minds on spiritual matters. So we must have a sentiment or opinion about spiritual things.

I remember the movie series *"Oh, God!"* in which George Burns played the part of God. In the second movie (*Oh, God! Book II*, 1980) God came to an 11-year-old girl and wanted her to be his marketing manager for the whole earth. She came up with the slogan that was going to get the campaign going, and that slogan was "Think God." She had her friends in grade school make up posters and put them in shop windows. The next morning all over town, on the church notice board (much to the disgust of the minister), on the school blackboards, and in many other places it said, "Think God," "Think God." When the movie was shown on our local television on a Sunday evening, the next morning the same thing happened in our schools too. On all the blackboards was "Think God," "Think God." That's what we must do—"Think God." Set your thoughts and opinions on things above.

You see, the problem is that while we *are* Christians, we do live in a material world. We are not yet in heaven—we're here on earth and we handle material things every day. The way to live how God wants us to in a hostile world is to get the eyes of your mind off those limiting material circumstances and get them on our opulent God. Get your minds on spiritual values where there are no limits. That's why Paul says here, "seek" and "set"—two things that we have to do. Seek and set. That's the message of verses 1 and 2.

And then in verse 3 it says *"For you died..."* Did you know you're already dead? That's what the Bible says. *"Reckon yourselves to be dead"* (Romans 6:11). You are dead and *"your life is hidden with Christ in God."* That's how God views you. The old Peter Wade is dead. And all God's people said "Amen!" You died. And what did God do? God gave you new life and hid it with Christ. It's a hidden life. That's why the world can't figure out what makes us tick, because it's hidden from them. It's a life that's hidden in God. It says your life is hid with Christ in God. And since that's where the center of my life is, then I'm in good company. I'm doing what J. Paul Getty said to do in his book *How to be Rich.* I'm rubbing shoulders with those who are successful, and there's nobody more successful than our God and Father. There's the security we have. *"For you died* [the text is past tense] *and your life is hidden with Christ in God."* (Wings hide you — for protection —

Then in verse 4, *"When Christ who is our life..."* There is the source of our life. Write the word "source" in the margin. The hidden life is actually Christ. He is our life. That is why Paul said in Galatians 2:20 that it was not him living his life. He said, *"It is no longer I who live, but Christ lives in me."* Christ is our life. When we start living life from a Christ viewpoint, then you are living it in God's way even though you might be in a hostile world. Now you have the answer to that question "How can I fly like an eagle when I have to work with turkeys all week?" Easy, because you have Christ in you, and Christ is on top of the world, and he wants you to be on top of the world too.

In just four verses we have simple yet profound truth: *seek* the heavenly, *set* the mind, and know the *source.*

18

Put to Death and Put Off

Colossians 3:5-11

"Therefore put to death your members which are earthly: fornica-tion, uncleanness, passion, evil desire, and covetousness, which is idolatry" (verse 5). Write the word "slay" in the margin. Now you might wonder what a positive teacher is doing talking about negative things like that. Well, let me illustrate this way. We have to pull the weeds out of the garden in order that the positive plants might grow. It doesn't matter how positive our ministry is, the Bible still says there are some negative, limiting, self-denigrating aspects of life that we have to deal with and get them out of our circumstances.

God has rules. To the Jewish people He gave the Ten Com-mandments, not the ten suggestions! To New Testament believers God says if you do this, this, and this you will have success. God says if you'll throw that off and throw that off, then you will remove the blockage that's holding you down. Let's look at some of His rules. Verse 5 gives a list of what we might call sensual sins: fornication, uncleanness, lustful passion, evil desire, and covetousness, which is idolatry. *"Because of these things the wrath of God is coming on the sons of disobedience, 7In which you also once walked, when you were living in them"* (verses 6-7). There was a time when your nature allowed those earthly things to blossom, but now you've become a Christian. Those things no longer belong. They will just keep you down. They will keep you in self-perpetuating poverty in its widest sense. While we still have the ability to engage in all those activities, we should no longer have the desire to do so, because we're marching to a different tune now that we are Christians.

So the Word says to slay, to mortify (KJV), to put to death those sensual things. Treat them as if they're already dead. Treat them as if they have no place in your life whatsoever. Consider them dead. If any of those things cross your mind, toss out the thought. That is a very important step on the road to success. And it is not only those sensual sins but verse 8 says that there are social sins you also must put off (underline those words "put off"). *"But now you yourselves are to put off all these: anger, wrath, malice, slander, and foul language from your mouth."* The word picture is that of clothing. When you go to bed at night, you "put off" your clothes. You take them off. This list of sins has to do with our actions with other people and bad reactions we have concerning others.

"Put off... anger", for example. Occasionally you might do something stupid and make yourself mad, but usually it is somebody else that pulls your string. Someone else flicks the switch and causes you to "crack a fruity", as my boys used to say. You make a display of your intense dislike for the situation or person. "Wrath" is another word for fury, harshness. "Malice" is ill thought, ill feeling towards other people. "Blasphemy", evil speaking, dragging another person's reputation down. "Foul

language" or "abusive language" is filthy communication (KJV).

Then verse 9: *"Do not lie to one another..."* Oh, but there are white lies and gray lies and black lies!" Are there? Who said? It doesn't say that in the Bible. It says "do not lie." And why not? *"... seeing that you have put off the old humanity with its practices."* Notice that the first "put off" we underlined in verse 8 is something that you have to do. You take an action. You take those clothes off that are no longer fitting for a child of God. Yet verse 9 says *"you have put off"* (underline those words). You have already done it. It's signed, sealed, and finished. You have put off the old humanity, or the old man. You have already put it off as far as God is concerned. It's done. You are no longer controlled by the old. You have put off the old humanity with its practices and *"have put on..."* (underline those words). It's already done.

"And have put on the new humanity..." (verse 10a). You have already done it. It's already part of your makeup. What God is saying to us is to not just to declare that it has happened but to demonstrate it. We demonstrate it by getting rid of those negatives out of our lives and replacing them with the beautiful, productive positives, full of potential, that God has for us in his Word. So let's put off all of these things.

"And have put on the new humanity, which is being renewed in full knowledge according to the image of him who created him, [11]where there cannot be Greek nor Jew, circumcised nor uncircumcised, barbarian, Scythian, slave nor free, but Christ is all, and in all" (verses 10-11). So not only do we have to seek, set, know the source, and slay the earthly but we need to strengthen our knowledge of the Christ that is resident within us. You see, man was *formed* in

God's image. Man was *deformed* by sin when Adam committed high treason and Satan came in and took over. But the provision has been made for man to be *transformed* back into God's image once again. That image is the Christ that is within us.

It says there is neither "Greek nor Jew." Nationality makes no difference. There is neither "circumcised nor uncircumcised," which refers to religion. The Jews were circumcised; those of the other religions were not. Religion makes no difference. "Barbarian or Scythian," which refers to culture. Barbarians are foreigners, that is how the word was used. Scythians were considered the most barbaric of the barbarians, "savages" is one way you could translate it. So differences in culture have no impact here. "Slave [bond] nor free." Your political or economic standing has nothing to do with it, or whether you are an employer or an employee. In Galatians 3:28 it even goes on to say neither "male nor female," so gender differences have nothing to do with this, *"for you are all one in Christ Jesus,"* it says in Galatians. And here in Colossians it says, *"Christ is all, and in all,"* so we strengthen the effect of the Christ within. I could teach for hours on "Christ is all, and in all"! We read earlier in Colossians that Christ is everything (see our seventh chapter). Here we read that Christ is all-compassing, and he "occupies the whole sphere of human life and permeates all its developments" (Lightfoot).

So how do we strengthen the effect of Christ within? We set our mind on things above. We seek those things which are above. We recognise our source. We slay the earthly. We strengthen our knowledge of the Christ within. Those are very powerful statements. We must be willing to be different. Anybody can go with the tide of popular opinion. What Christianity needs and what your country needs are people who will stand up and make a success out of life. When people get rid of the negatives and demonstrate the positive, then people look around and say "I sure want what they've got." We need people who not only say "I believe it," but who will demonstrate it for God's glory.

19

Your New Wardrobe

Colossians 3:12-14

In the previous section we were told to put off certain negative, limiting influences in our lives. Now we are told to put on certain things, and I think we can relate to this. Most of us actually spend quite a bit of money on our clothes. I can remember when I was growing up as a teenager, living in England at the time, just 30 miles north of London. My elder sister and mother would go to London to buy a new wardrobe for my sister, who had reached those years when she was very fashion conscious. She would complain for weeks that she "didn't have a rag to wear," even though her wardrobe was full. So they would go to London and would buy all these new clothes in tune with whatever the family budget was at the time, but by the time they got back on the train to Chelmsford Station my sister would have swapped those clothes with our mother and it would start all over again! There are certain clothes for certain situations and Paul uses this illustration in Colossians chapter 3.

In Colossians 3:5 we were told to slay or put to death certain activities in our lives. And then in verse 8 it said, *"But now you yourselves are to put off all these."* You can see in the first nine verses that we have a wardrobe full of some very limiting situations, things that we should not have active in our lives. In verse 11 we are encouraged with the fact that since we have Christ in us, since Christ is all and in all, then we have no need for those activities in our lives. We should be willing to be different. We should throw out some of those old unwanted clothes and fill up the wardrobe with some better things that we need to put on.

Now, in verses 12 to 14, Paul continues the illustration of clothing. I don't know about you, but I don't wear everything that I need for any situation that I will run across. For example, I like to spend time on the beach when the weather is good. I used to go for a run every day. Now, I don't wear my swimwear under my suit and I don't wear my running shorts and top under all this sartorial splendor, and you don't either. You dress for whatever situation or activity you are involved in. As I was thinking about this passage it seemed to me that we could also illustrate this with keys. We have a bunch of keys, and we select the right key for the right occasion; then we have the ability to get into anywhere we want to go. We have a lot of keys but we only use the one we need at a particular point in time. And I think that is the teaching that we see here in verses 12 to 14—the situations we run across and the right keys to handle them.

Verse 12 say *"Put on then, as God's chosen ones, holy and loved..."* "Put on"—underline that in your Bible, because this is a command not a suggestion. "Put on" indicates an action you must do as an outworking of grace. God is saying to you to put on these things because you are chosen of God, "the elect of God" (KJV). He chose you because he loved you—that's what the Bible teaches.

Notice what God says in Deuteronomy chapter 7, where He describes why he took particular care of the nation of Israel. *"God did not set his love upon you, nor choose you, because you were more in number than any people; for you were the fewest of all people:* **8***But because God loved you, and because he would keep the oath which he had sworn to your fathers"* (verses 7-8a). So even back in Old Testament times God blessed the nation of Israel because God loved them. And I could go to New Testament verses where it says that God loves every human being. The administration has changed and God is working with individuals and not nations, so God loves everybody. He chose us not because we were handsome or because we were brilliant. He chose us because He loved us. He saw in us potential and He loved us. So that's where this passage starts. We are chosen of God, we are holy, that is, set apart, and we are loved. If you don't get anything else out of this teaching, have these words ringing in your ears—"You are loved." There is at least one person who loves you. And if you have more than one then you are extremely blessed. You are greatly loved. At least one person loves you, and that person is God.

Seven new garments

The first new garment is "hearts of compassion," "bowels of mercy" (KJV). *"Put on... hearts of compassion."* Do you understand what compassion is? It means that instead of standing on your rights or letting somebody else worry about a situation, on occasion you show some mercy and do some random act of compassion. Notice that these first seven garments and the eighth outer garment, the master garment, all relate to our dealings with other people. They relate to those who are around us. Put on compassion. Use it. There will be an occasion this week when you need to use compassion.

Secondly it says, *"put on... kindness."* Be kind to somebody. It doesn't take long. Sometimes it doesn't take a lot of effort. Think of some way in which you can be kind to somebody this week. I remember a wonderful advertisement on television some years ago. It was about two business men with their briefcases rushing into the airport in order to catch their plane. A little boy with his jigsaw puzzle and toys unfortunately happens to get knocked by one of the briefcases, and his puzzle and toys went all over the floor. One man turned around to come back and pick them up, and the other man said, "Oh God! What are you doing?" And when he stopped and picked up the toys, the little boy said, "Thank you, God." What a great example. Spend a little kindness, it helps make the world go around. It's one of those positive keys to Christian living that you can use.

Thirdly, in verse 12, it speaks about *"humility"*, or "humbleness of mind" (KJV). Of course, all these things start in the mind anyway. Be humble. There are a lot of people who are proud of their humbleness. That is, they attempt to make a display of their humbleness and become quite a pain in the neck by doing so. The Bible says to *"put on... humility."* Remember who you are. Don't have a high opinion of yourself. Don't be a legend in your own mind. Be humble. Remember that you are a unique human being that God has made, but remember also your fellow human beings are unique too! They too have self esteem. They too have great potential, so be humble and just thank God for the light that you have received so far along life's road.

The next garment is meekness, *"put on... meekness."* This is the one that everybody complains about. Should a Christian let everybody walk all over them? No! Jesus talked about meekness, and yet I would remind you that He went into the Temple, got hold of a whip, and cleaned that place up in a typical Rambo fashion. So what is meekness? Meekness is power under control. The Message Bible paraphrases it as "quiet strength," and many other translations use "gentleness." The Greek word is used in three different situations. It is used first of a soothing wind, say a nice cool breeze on the beach at Waikiki in the evening. It is also used of a healing medicine. And it is used of a colt that has been broken. Yet in all those things there is power but it's under control. There's power in the wind to cool. There's power in the medicine to heal, and there's power in the colt that is controlled. Meekness is power under control. You have incredible power. You have power to bless and power to hurt people. You have power in the words you say. Words can work wonders and words can work blunders. Let's use this power but let's keep it under control. That's what meekness is all about.

Now we come to the fifth garment, *"put on... longsuffering."* We've all had to do that, haven't we? The Greek word actually means long temper. Now you can understand that. You know what it is when a person has a short temper, right? We say short because we use the figure of the fuse. The fuse is short and if you light that fuse the explosion is rapid. And what we should have is a long fuse on our temper. We should be long-tempered, long-suffering towards other people. They can't hurt you. The only thing that can happen to you is that you give power to their actions to have an effect on you. Just like circumstances. Circumstances can have no effect upon you unless you give them power. That's a psychological principle. Other people can't hurt you. I know other people can say things about you but it's your reaction that will hurt you and it won't worry them one little bit. Be longsuffering. Be long-tempered. Many translations use the word "patient."

Next we have *"put on... forbearance,"* number six. *"Bearing with one another"* (verse 13a)—yes, haven't we done that a lot? The Greek word means to hold back. Hold back yourself when you feel you need to give that person a large piece of your mind. Have forbearance. "Some mornings I wake up grumpy; other mornings I let him sleep in!"

Number seven is forgiveness. *"... and forgiving one another, if anyone should have a complaint against any: even as Christ forgave you, so also do"* (verse 13b). Forgiveness. How much has Christ forgiven you? The answer has to be everything. And it says even as Christ forgave you, so also do to others. Let's be forgiving one to another. I have noticed that even in a church situation people do things that hurt at times and we have to forgive them. Sometimes people do things based on false information. Sometimes they do things because they just haven't thought it through from another person's point of view. Let's be forgiving. Let's not start a World War over the situation. Be forgiving, let it settle down, because it's your happiness and your successful life that really is at stake.

The outer master garment

Now, verse 14, *"and above all..."* What does that mean? On top of the seven we have already discussed. Using the clothing illustration, it would mean having already put on all these undergarments, put on over all of them this outer garment. *"And above all these things put on love, which holds everything together"* (verse 14). Love is the Greek word "agapao," the God kind of love. Put it on. Using the keys illustration, I call this the master key. If you haven't got room to carry all eight keys around, just take the key of love. Love fixes all of them. Love takes care of compassion. Love takes care of kindness, humbleness, meekness, long-suffering, forbearance, and forgiveness. Above all these things use the key of love. *God Kind of Love*

Some of you might remember the hit song written in 1965 by Hal David, "What the world needs now is love, sweet love." That is true. And what we really need is more love in action. We need more people showing forth their love. God has given us a special kind of love. It's a love that can love the unlovely. As William Booth, the founder of the Salvation Army, used to say, "Go for souls, and go for the worst." His attitude was that it was God's love in his heart that enabled him to love the alcoholic in the street gutter, to love the prostitute, to love all those who were really what we call "down and outs." The same kind of love is needed also for those that we could call the "up and outs", the yuppies and geeks, and the rich and famous. God's love is in our hearts according to Romans 5:5, so put on love, put it into practice. Now let me say it again. This is not a suggestion, it's a command. If you want to live God's way in a negative world, then start seeing life through the eyes of love.

When I teach this passage live, I use a slide of a man standing in front of a wardrobe, with two doors open, trying to make up his mind what to wear. One side is labelled "Put Off" and the other side "Put On". I like that diagram because it really teaches us something. Here's this fellow thinking, "What shall I wear today?" You see, the clothes on the negative side of the wardrobe are still around. If we so desire we can put them on. The decision is up to you and to me. God has given us help in the decision-making. God has given us power to make the right decisions but every day, in fact, every moment of every day, you have to decide shall I explode or shall I handle this with love. Shall I give them a piece of my mind, or shall I just say nothing? You make the decision. You decide what you put on, or to put it another way, to use the master key of love.

20

Three Personal Keys

Colossians 3:15-17

Let's continue in Colossians 3 with three personal keys to use. Verses 12, 13, and 14 had to do with situations with other people. Now we find three keys which have to do with our personal life. Verse 15, *"And let..."* The word "let" is used five times in Colossians and indicates something you have to do. Verse 16, *"Let..."* It's something else you have to do. And in verse 17, *"And whatever you do..."* So these instructions are put on our shoulders very clearly and specifically. These are situations in our personal lives about which we have to do certain things.

First, verse 15, *"And let the peace of Christ..."* (The KJV reads "the peace of God" but most translations render it "the peace of Christ" or "the peace that comes from Christ".) Verse 16, *"Let the word of Christ..."* Verse 17, *"... do everything in the name of the Lord Jesus,"* so Christ is in the immediate context. And as we have seen, Christ is at the center of everything (verse 11).

Let's go back to verse 15. *"And let the peace of Christ act as umpire in your hearts, to which you were also called in one body. And be thankful."* The word "rule" (KJV) is an athletic term. We've come across it before in Colossians 2:18. It means to umpire. Let the peace of Christ be the umpire in your heart. Whenever there's a situation that you don't know what to do about, let the peace of Christ determine the outcome. Let the peace of Christ flow. Accept the umpire's decision and the solution will flow along the right line. The Word says "let the peace of Christ act as umpire." Let it be the decision maker. Let it be the motivating force to help your decisions in all of life's situations.

Jesus himself said before he left this earth, *"Peace I leave with you; my peace I give to you. Not as the world gives do I give to you. Let not your heart be troubled, neither let it be afraid"* (John 14:27). Jesus left peace with you and if there's ever a time when people need that tranquility of mind, it is right now in our present society. The pressures are enormous but the peace is strong enough to rule. *"... to which you were also called in one body."* The reason we gather together in the Body of Christ (a term used for the church universal) is so that peace can flow among this group of people. There should be no one in this group to whom we don't want to talk. In fact, perhaps today might be a good time to find somebody you haven't said something to for a week or two and at least say, "Hello. How you going?" Verse 15 concludes with *"And be thankful."* This refers to your calling—be thankful you are a member of the Body of Christ, the Church. Your local fellowship is your primary care organization.

Now the second personal key, verse 16. *"Let the word of Christ dwell in you richly..."* (I believe the *"in all wisdom"* belongs to the next phrase). Remember, you do the letting! The word "dwell" is a beautiful word, because it means to make itself at home in your heart. "Let the word of Christ be making its home in you richly" (Concordant). "The word of Christ" can be translated as the word "delivered by Christ" or as the word "about Christ." Does it feel comfortable to know the Word is within? This is not saying just to take "a verse a day to keep the devil away", but it says let it dwell "richly." How am I going to live and grow in Christ in a hostile world? I'm going to fill my mind with God's Word and when situations arise I have a foundation in the form of principles. These are like filters. All the information, all the ideas that come my way I filter through the Word that is within me, and that helps me decide which way to go. Some things I can delete immediately. Some things I can say, "Look, that's going to hurt somebody else. I will not go down that road. There's got to be a better way to do it." Put it through the filter of the Word. You will only be able to do that when the Word dwells in you "richly."

Then verse 16 continues by saying we should *"in all wisdom teach and admonish one another; singing in grace in your hearts to God, in psalms, hymns, spiritual songs."* Now you know why we sing! I've had people come up to me and want to leave out all the songs and just have the Bible teaching. Well, I'm sure the idea is based on a very noble purpose, but the Bible does instruct us to sing. I think there's great value in true Christian music, because those songs fall into two categories. Some songs we sing to other people, to encourage one another. And other songs are songs of praise that we sing to our God. So we keep that as a necessary part of our celebration together. Sing psalms, hymns, spiritual songs. Not surprisingly, it doesn't say anything about the style of singing, like rock and roll or rap, but we'll ask the Lord about that when we get to heaven! So we should have singing. It is a necessary part of the Christian life and it doesn't finish on Sunday, because songs drop back into your mind during the week. There's great value in music described here.

And finally in verse 17, *"And whatever you do, in word or deed, do all things in the name of the Lord Jesus, giving thanks to God the Father through him."* Do everything in the name of or in the authority of the Lord Jesus. If what you're doing cannot be done in the name of Christ, then don't do it. That is how we should approach life. If you cannot put the name of the Lord Jesus in place of your name in an activity, then that activity is wrong. Whatever you do, do it in the authority of the name of the Lord Jesus, giving thanks to God through him.

So, what does this passage teach us? Very simply, in God's sight we're all dressed up and we do have somewhere to go! We have the joy of living a positive, prosperous successful Christian life.

Let's look at the wardrobe just one last time. Put off all these things: anger, wrath, malice, slander, and foul language and come alive. Put on hearts of compassion, kindness, humility, meekness, longsuffering, forbearance, forgiveness, and above all put on love. So there's your spiritual wardrobe. You have the keys. Bind them on your belt or in your purse. Use them this week. Let's make it practical. There's no sense me teaching you Bible knowledge if you're not going to go out and make it work. This week, perhaps even before this day is over, you'll find an opportunity to use some of those keys. Use them and then you will live and grow in Christ in a hostile world.

21

Spouses: Submit and Sacrifice

Colossians 3:18-19

In our journey through the book of Colossians we have arrived at Colossians chapter 3 and verse 18. Home is where you let your hair down, and home is sometimes the place where we forget to apply the positive principles of God's Word. What we have learned so far in Colossians is that faith in Christ can really change individuals. Up to this verse we've seen the truth from an individual viewpoint, but now God seems to find it important to show us that faith in His way can change marriages, can change child raising, can change job situations. It is interesting that God saw these three areas as needing special comment. Everything we will see in this passage is based on what we have already seen up to this point in Colossians. For example, we saw in Colossians 3:17, *"And whatever you do, in word or deed, do all things in the name of the Lord Jesus, giving thanks to God the Father through him."* The "do all things" includes the marriage, the family, and the job situation.

It is not new information to say that it was God who set up the family unit. The family is still the basic unit of our society. Confucius said the strength of a nation derives from the integrity of the home, and he was only echoing what the Bible has said.

Wives

So let's look into verse 18 and look first at the verbs. *"Wives, submit to your husbands, as is fitting in the Lord."* A verb is a word of action, and in verse 18 the first verb we run across is "submit." That is a powerful word. Some of the wives reading this really want to know what it means. I've looked it up in all the modern translations. I've checked it out in the Greek text, and "submit" means to submit. So, we should have no problem with the word itself, but how do we apply it? That's the question.

It is actually a military word and perhaps this will help your understanding of it. It merely means to arrange in ranks— privates, sergeant-majors, lieutenants, colonels, generals, and so on. If you apply that picture, the private is in fact as good a person as the general. There's no difference in the humanity of a person because they have a different rank. And that is what we must understand in this verse about wives. There is no difference between a wife and a husband except in rank. Wives are still unique human individuals who have tremendous potential, just like husbands. In the military everyone is needed in order to accomplish the victory.

Now keep that in mind as we come to this verse which says *"Wives, submit to your husbands..."* The current trend of our society is to have equality among the sexes, and I'm all for that. The only difference between the two partners is one of rank. The husband has more responsibilities than the wife. We'll see that in a moment. There is a best-selling novel titled *First Among Equals*, set in the political world We also know the old saying that everyone is equal but some are more equal than others. In a marriage situation there are two unique, beautiful human beings who have agreed to link their lives together. And each one has a part to play. Right throughout my ministry I've taught that marriage is at least a 51/49 relationship, because that's biblical.

In Colossians, wives get the first mention. That is not because they needed it more than the husbands. It's perhaps because Christianity did something tremendous for women. In fact, we owe it to Christianity for the state women have today in Western nations. Back in the days of the New Testament women had a very lowly rank. They were one step above a slave, and then along came the good news of Christ that said every person has potential. Every person is loved by God. Every person has a place to fulfill. It's important for women to get that message. The situation did not change overnight but it did gradually, as people believed the teaching of the gospel. Where Christianity has come the place of women has been lifted in society. Today we can look at the Middle East and see that where Christianity is suppressed so are the rights of women.

"Wives,submit to your husbands, as is fitting in the Lord." When God set up the family unit He said that it will work successfully in a Christian home when the wife submits herself to her husband. However, there is one thing that comes prior to that, and that is first for the wife to submit herself to the Lord. That's what it means as is fitting in the Lord. If wives have submitted themselves to the Lord then they won't have any problem submitting themselves to their husbands. This does not give the husband the right to be the dictator in the family. They have the right of headship but not dictatorship. That's why I still

say after more than 50 years of marriage that the ideal relationship is 51/49, and each one has a part to play. So wives, submit
yourself to your own husbands as is fitting, as is proper, as is your
obligation in the Lord.

Husbands

Now, having dealt with the wives, let's take on the husbands.
What are husbands supposed to do? *"Husbands, love your wives,
and do not be harsh with them"* (verse 19). "Oh," you husbands say,
"I already follow that. That's the easy part. I've got that solved."
Just be careful what you are reading here. It is not what you might
think, husbands. The Greek word for "love" is not *phileo* which we
incorporate into English place names like Philadelphia, which
means brotherly love. *Phileo* is the normal human kind of love
which is why you got married in the first place. Love is the itchings
of the heart that you can't get at to scratch, as my father often said.
This verse uses another word, *agapao,* which is exclusively used
for the uncompromising love of God resident within the believer.
That distinction is important because it's a different kind of love.
The *phileo* kind of love is really a selfish love. You are loving that
other person because you want to get a benefit from them. In this
verse it is God's love being manifested, being evidenced through
you as a husband, because you want to benefit your wife.
*"Husbands, be loving your wives with a divine love which impels you
to deny yourselves for their benefit..."* (Wuest).

Keep your finger in Colossians and look at the parallel
passage in Ephesians chapter 5. *"Husbands, love your own wives,
just as Christ also loved the church and gave Himself for her, ²⁶in
order that He might sanctify her, cleansing her by the washing of*

119

water by the word, ²⁷*that He might present her to Himself a glorious church, not having spot or wrinkle or any such thing, but that she should be holy and blameless.* ²⁸*So husbands ought to love their own wives as their own bodies; he that loves his own wife loves himself"* (Ephesians 5:25-28). Sacrifice is inherent in the love Christ has for the church universal, and it's the husband's responsibility in the marriage.

Now the problem with teaching this is that we can merely rearrange our prejudices, and we use both of these words as a club on each other. "Peter Wade said you've got to sacrifice yourself for me." "Yes, but Peter also said you've got to submit." That's not doing it in love, folk. You have to make this thing work and it can work. There are enough examples around to show that we can go against the trend of present society where one in three marriages ends in divorce. We can prove to the world that with God's love within each of us, with individual faith in God, marriage can work. Marriage is a wonderful thing. I don't like to call marriage an institution. Who wants to live in an institution? Marriage is a beautiful relationship between two people and God knew that we needed specific help in that. In addition to putting on the grace clothes or those positive keys that we talked about earlier, and in addition to letting the peace of Christ be the umpire and letting the Word dwell in us, we need to take those two key words, "submit" and "sacrifice" and make our marriages work.

22

Children and Parents

Colossians 3:20-21

Children

In Colossians 3:20-21 we come to the minors, our dear, darling children. It just seems that the natural result of marriage is children, and children are a *"heritage from the Lord,"* it says in Psalm 127:3. It goes on to say that they are like arrows and *"blessed is the man whose quiver is filled with them!"* (verse 5). Well, that may surprise you! The home is a unit where there's a husband, a wife, and children—a nuclear family. There are special words in this Colossian passage to the children as well as to the parents.

"Children, obey your parents in everything, for this is pleasing in the Lord" (verse 20). I do not want to set my children up as any paragons of childhood behaviour, because my children were typical PKs—Preacher's Kids. Preacher's kids have the reputation of being the worst. Preacher's kids can get into trouble, and when they do everybody knows about it. When we moved to America with the family in the 1960s, at that time in Australia children were still being brought up in an English manner, if I might use

that term. Parents still had control over their children. In America children were being allowed free expression; that was the current philosophy. Now I believe in free expression with children, so long as I am the one who is expressing it! I'm just old-fashioned enough to believe that a pat on the back develops character, so long as it's low enough, and early enough, and hard enough. "Spare the rod and spoil the child", and so forth. When we arrived in America we met Bishop K.C. Pillai, who was a bishop from the Indian Orthodox Church and a noted expert on Oriental customs. He came up to me and commended Vivien and myself on how our children were behaving in public, because he could see the difference. He had lived in England for a few years and then in America for 20 years, and he could see that even though our children were quite normal and got into all the usual things that kids do, nevertheless it was quite obvious they had been taught to obey. *"Train up a child in the way he should go. Even when he is old he will not depart from it"* (Proverbs 22:6).

And now think of those adolescent years when you will need to remember all these verses, the years when some folk say that you ought to bury your kids at 8 and dig them up again at 18! In those middle years if they don't obey you as parents they are not going to obey authority and we will have a continual spread of lawlessness throughout the land. What is the problem? Someone's mother hasn't taught those teenagers to obey. Someone's father hasn't trained that adolescent. This is what life is all about, for there is no freedom without fences.

I read an oft-told story about General William Booth, founder of the Salvation Army. In 1877 in Leicester, England, he was asked by the authorities to conduct the funeral of a man named John Starkey. This man had murdered his wife and was brought up before the courts, convicted and hanged. Around the graveside was the greatest collection of criminals you could imagine. Booth was not too sure how as a preacher he should handle this mean-looking crowd with the gospel of God's love. He got up and caught their attention with his first words. He said, "John Starkey did not have a praying mother," and he had that crowd in his hands. In a world of great ideas from experts like Dr. Spock and Dr. Phil, let's remember God created the family. God has given the instructions on how to handle the family and children who do not obey naturally. We have to teach them to obey their parents. In what areas? In everything! *"Children, obey your parents in everything, for this is pleasing in the Lord"* (verse 20). What's the motivation? It will please the Lord.

Parents

"Fathers, do not provoke your children, lest they become discouraged" (verse 21). I know mothers also have plenty to do with children. In fact, too often only mothers bring up our children. I read of a survey that said in one small town in America they tried to discover how much time fathers spent with their sons—it averaged out at 37 seconds a day. Does that say something to you? You need to make time with your kids, fathers. The word "fathers" in the text can be translated "parents"—"Parents, do not provoke..." Look at the verbs. Put a circle around these verbs and they'll stand out for you. Verse 18, wives "submit"—a verb. Verse 19, husbands "love". Verse 20, children "obey". Verse 21, parents "provoke" not. That is the only verb that is expressed negatively in

this passage. One translation has it as "do not irritate" them (Amplified). So there are your verbs. In marriage, submit and sacrifice. With children, obey and encourage, two sides of the one coin.

One of the problems that I've observed is that we parents are so inconsistent, and so we discourage our kids. We go from one moment of being totally permissive, letting them get away with anything, and on the other hand we come down like a ton of bricks on them. They wonder why we let them go that far into left field and then we throw them that far into right field. Don't irritate your kids. Don't provoke them. You see, the responsibility is on our shoulders in bringing up those children. They are God's gift to us. They are wonderful to have. They give us a lot of joy, a lot of love, and sometimes a little bit of pain. It's our responsibility to bring them up. We are responsible for them. So, *"Parents, do not provoke your children, lest they become discouraged."* If they don't get their ego strength from the home, they'll get it from the gutter. It is up to you and to me as to which it is going to be. So there are the two things for the family life: Children obey, parents provoke not.

23

Christ in the Workplace

Colossians 3:22-25; 4:1

Slaves

We move on to the workplace—slaves and masters. *"Slaves, obey in everything your masters according to the flesh..."* (verse 22). And what is the first verb for slaves? "Obey." Let's put a circle around that. Slaves obey in everything. Half of the population in those days were slaves, and the best translation of the word here is "slaves." The word "masters" is the same word as for "lords," but its preferable to use "masters" here as Christian slaves had Christ as Lord. Now Paul did not advocate protest. There's no mention of strike action about the situation. Slaves had absolutely no rights. They were considered common chattel. If the slave's master wanted to beat them to death he had the legal right to do so.

Paul did not advocate protest marches. He did not advocate rebellion against authority. He did not advocate overthrowing the system. What he advocated was working with individuals, and he starts with slaves and then masters. It is only as we change as individuals that we change the nation. You can legislate all you like. Australia is said to be the country with more legislation than any Western nation. Yet we still follow the same trends that the rest of the world do. We still have the same high crime rate. We still have the same drug problem. We still have the same percentage of marriages breaking up. We still have the hordes of single parents, and so on. Legislation has never changed anything. Changing the individual is what will change society.

So the Bible says, *"Slaves, obey in everything your masters according to the flesh, not by way of eye-service as people-pleasers, but in sincerity of heart, fearing the Lord.* ²³*Whatever you do, work heartily, as to the Lord and not to men, knowing that from the Lord you will receive the reward of the inheritance.* ²⁴*Serve the Lord Christ"* (verses 22-24). When you are working for your master you *are* serving the Lord Christ! That is who you are working for. So don't work "heartily" or "willingly" just because the boss has got his eye on you. Do it because you're doing it as to the Lord. *"For the one doing wrong will be paid back for the wrong he has done, and there are no exceptions"* (verse 25). It is likely that this verse refers to both slaves and masters. That is a sobering thought.

Masters

Then in chapter 4 and verse 1, *"Masters, give to your slaves what is just and fair, knowing that you also have a Master in heaven."* Here's another case where the chapter break is not helpful. Let us circle the verb "give." What are masters to give? Justice and fairness. Slaves have no rights, so masters are being told to treat them in a humane way. Masters, be fair and honest to them. The word "give" or "provide" means to render from the master's own resources. The verse concludes with a sobering thought for masters to remember that they have God as their Master.

Let's conclude these marriage, parenting, workplace passages with this thought. The heart of every problem is the problem of the heart. The problem of the marriage is a problem of the hearts of people. The problems in the family with children are problems of the heart. The problems in the workplace are problems of the heart. We must work on the hearts of people, and the best way to do that is by introducing them to Christ, by holding up Christ as preeminent in everything. *"Christ is all, and in all"* (Colossians 3:11).

24

The Power of Speech

Colossians 4:2-3a

Our journey in Colossians has brought us to chapter 4 and verse 2. We have seen that we have to be willing to be different from everybody else. In chapter 3 we were told to put off the clothes that were no longer needed for our positive Christian life and then we were told to put on certain other clothes, which I suggested could also be seen as keys for positive living. And then we saw that we have to be positive at home, in the marriage, parenting our children, and also in the workplace with masters and servants.

Now we are encouraged to learn the power of speech, and it is a very powerful thing. A judge can just say a few words and a man's life is totally changed. He's either free and can go out to live a normal life and not be concerned with the charges that were laid against him, or he can be convicted and jailed for some time. Just a few words can change a person's life. You can visit your doctor who has performed all those tests on you, and you say "Okay, doctor, what's the diagnosis?" And you can respond with great rejoicing in your heart or incredible despair as to what the future may hold, depending on your understanding of God's

Word. All it takes is just a few words. There's tremendous power in the power of speech.

Words are powerful tools and in this passage we have quite a few statements about the power of speech, using words like "utterance", "speak," "speech." May I first remind you about another passage in the Word of God. James chapter 3 has a whole section about the tongue and what a powerful member of the body it is. *"Consider that we put bits in horses' mouths that they may obey us, and we guide their whole body. ⁴Consider also the ships: although they are so large and are driven by fierce winds, they are guided by a very small rudder wherever the impulse of the helmsman intends. ⁵Even so the tongue is a little member and it boasts great things. See how great a forest a little fire kindles!"* (James 3:3-5).

The tongue can put you in some awkward situations and it can put you into some very positive situations. The choice is yours. The tongue is likened to a fire, and we know fire can warm. Fire can cook our meals for us, but fire can also destroy our homes! The tongue is just like that. It can destroy people. It can really kill situations. But the Bible also says it can be like a fruitful tree. It can allow situations to develop and blossom. It is also pictured as a fountain. Good can come forth via the tongue if we so desire.

Using the tongue to pray

There are four applications of the power of speech in Colossians chapter 4, and we'll look at these as we go along. First of all to pray. *"Continue steadfastly in prayer, watching in it with thanksgiving. At the same time, praying also for us..."* (Colossians 4:2-3a). There are several things there about prayer, and I think it's interesting that the apostle starts the discussion on speech with the subject of prayer. It doesn't start with you talking to your wife or husband or talking to others. The most important, the most valuable application of the power of speech is to talk to God. As someone has well said, "If you're having trouble with prayer, then talk to God about it!" That will solve the problem. Talk to God. I believe very strongly in a positive approach to prayer, having written and taught about this on many occasions.

"Continue steadfastly [perseveringly] in prayer." That is, give constant attention to prayer. In other passages like I Thessalonians 5:17, we are told to "pray without ceasing." Now that doesn't mean that you walk around all day mumbling to yourself, because people will start wondering what's wrong upstairs. To be persevering in prayer is to give continual attention to it, to do it on many occasions, to do it whenever it comes to your mind, whenever there's a situation that looms big or small in your affairs. Pray about it, even if it is just a one-sentence prayer, even if it's never uttered by the lips but just thought in the mind. Give continual attention to prayer. Be constant. Continue perseveringly in prayer.

As I have taught elsewhere (e.g. *God's Principles and Your Potential*, page 176 ff.), prayer is a conversation, and a conversation involves two people. Prayer is not a one-way deal, like reading out of a prayer book. Prayer is a two-way conversation between two people who love each other. It's a love conversation, it really is our time of fellowship with God our Father. People say to me that Jesus spent half the night in prayer when he had a problem and shouldn't we spend at least that much time? Well, not necessarily! Why did Jesus spend half the night in prayer? Was it because Jesus had problems he couldn't handle? Was it because he was lacking power? No, the reason Jesus spent half the night in prayer was because he needed fellowship with his Father. It was a question of fellowship. We too need to constantly remember as we go through life that we and God are partners in the human condition. Drill that into your mind, and there is no better way of fellowship than talking to God. Let's be faithful. Let's give constant attention to prayer.

Then verse 2 also says *"watching in it* [prayer] *with thanksgiving"*—stay alert and intent. In the book of Nehemiah when they were rebuilding the walls of Jerusalem, Nehemiah said, *"And we prayed to our God and set a watch against them day and night"* (Nehemiah 4:9). So there's a suggestion here about prayer that we need to be alert to what is happening around us and make that the subject also of our prayers.

Then for the second time in the book of Colossians there is a mention of thanksgiving. Now I believe that prayer for a Christian believer, especially for one who understand the new creation in Christ and that Christ is in them, is a prayer of thanksgiving. If I am blessed with all spiritual blessing in heavenly places (Ephesians 1:3) and I am, if I am totally complete in Him (Colossians 2:10) and I am, then I don't have a list of requests. I have a list of thanks. It's a matter of me thanking God. Prayer in your normal language is a prayer of thanksgiving. Colossians 4:2 is encouraging us to continue to thank God. We need to keep this "attitude of gratitude" as some preachers have called it. There is no better way to do that than in the area of prayer. Be thankful!

Then in verse 3, *"Praying at the same time also for us..."*, so prayer is not just general. Prayer is specific. Now I was brought up in the church and I've heard the old timers pray all round the world and back again in 20 minutes! I've been to prayer meetings where you knew that one person would take the floor and would just seem to go on and on and on. So much of that kind of praying was to bless all the missionaries everywhere, bless all the starving children somewhere else. There was nothing very specific about it. Instead of blessing all the missionaries everywhere find one particular missionary that you want to focus your attention on and pray specifically! I believe that's what is being said here.

"Continue steadfastly in prayer... with thanksgiving" and while you are about it. say one for me too! And not just for Paul; there's Tychicus, Onesimus, Aristarchus, Mark, Justus, Epaphras, Luke and Demas—all mentioned in this passage. Pray for us! Let's be specific in our prayers, and a good way to pray for somebody else is thanksgiving. "Thank you, God, for little Adam. What a great kid he is." See Adam as perfect in health and mind, and be specific in regard to these situations. *"Praying... also for us."*

So the first application of the power of speech for the Christian believer is to give attention to prayer. I know I could teach all day on the matter of prayer. If you go into a Christian bookshop there are rows of books on the subject of prayer. Prayer is a key, an important key in the Christian life. "Continue steadfastly in prayer."

25

To Proclaim and Practice the Faith

Colossians 4:3b-6

Using the tongue to proclaim

Now let's move on further in this passage. We also use the power of speech to proclaim: *"that God may open to us a door for the word, to speak [proclaim] the mystery which is Christ, for which I have also been bound, that I may make it clear, as I ought to speak"* (verses 3b-4). What God is saying to us here is that there is always a right time, a right place, a right opportunity to share the Word of God. Saying the right word or sharing a book or an audio CD or a DVD at the right time could mean that a person will come to faith in God because of it. I can pray for doors to open that you might say the right thing and others can enjoy the same blessing you do.

Here in verse 3 prayer is requested specifically so Paul could proclaim "the mystery which is Christ" (Greek text). We saw what that was earlier: *"To whom [his saints] God willed to make known what are the riches of the glory of this mystery among the Gentiles, which is Christ in you, the expectation of glory"* (Colossians 1:27). *"To a full knowledge of the mystery of God the Father, and the Christ, [3]in whom are hidden all the treasures of wisdom and knowledge"*

(2:2-3). You are a container of Christ and because you are a container you are also an expressor of Christ to the world around you.

We use the power of speech to proclaim, to share the Word. And we listen and look for that right opportunity to share that Word. Paul certainly had many opportunities, even in prison. Philippians is also an epistle he wrote while under house arrest, and he says in Philippians 4:22, *"All the saints greet you, but especially those of the household of Caesar!"* He was chained to a soldier, as we read in another passage—that's what I call a captive audience! On the basis of what we read in Paul's letters, I'm totally confident that those soldiers heard about Christ. Paul used the opportunity he had. He didn't have an opening to hire the local theater for a night to have an evangelistic rally, but he did have a person who was chained to him.

He shared the truth with those men and before the end of the book of Philippians he talks of saints in Caesar's household! That is an incredible statement. Picture it today, evangelical Christians working in the Kremlin in Moscow or in the president's palace in Iran. That's what the situation was like. The Roman Empire at that time was opposed to Christianity, just as the Communist world is opposed to Christianity, and yet there were saints in Caesar's household. The saints were there because Paul used the opportunity he had to share the gospel even though he was in bonds. He certainly proclaimed or declared the "mystery which is Christ," and we should too.

So there is another good way to use the power of speech—proclaim God's Word. All of us can do this. It's not something that is set aside specifically for apostles or professional preachers.

Ordinary folk like us who live on the same street as other people, we can proclaim the positive truth of the Word of God.

Using the tongue in practice of the faith

Now Paul goes on further in verse 5, *"Walk in wisdom toward outsiders, redeeming the time."* So there is another way! Just because I like the "artful aid of alliteration," I've called this "practice." We need to practice our Christianity. A Christianity that is not practical is useless. It becomes a mind religion or a "pie in the sky" religion. I believe firmly in a positive, practical Christianity.

You might wonder what this has to do with speech, but you'll see in a moment. *"Walk in wisdom toward outsiders,"* that is, those who are outside of God's family. Now to "walk" here has nothing to do with a normal walk around the block. It means the way you live, your manner of life. "Behave yourself wisely" (Amplified), "Conduct yourselves with wisdom" (NET).

How do you walk in wisdom? You remember that you are an expression of Christ. People should not see you. They should see the Christ in you. That truth is going to determine my actions. Now I have had to recognize in life that there are some things I am not free to do, because with every freedom there are fences. I have a great love for the freedom in Christ and for that reason I do not legislate on others what I feel I could never do. However, you'll never rule in life unless you have regulations. So there are certain things I cannot do because I believe if I did them it would reflect on the Christ that I love and worship, and the Christ that is in me. I'm not teaching bondage. I am teaching liberty and freedom with self-control. Wherever there's freedom there has to be self-control.

The way you walk will determine how many people you turn to the ways of God. There's a song that says "They're not listening to your talk, they're looking at your walk." And that's very true. As teenagers we sang a chorus from the West Indies that had these lines, "Saying 'Amen' to the preacher is fine, If all through the week you let your light shine, I want to be more than a Sunday-go-to-meeting Christian." So first live the Christian life and "make the very most of the time and seizing (buying up) the opportunity" (Amplified). The same term is used in Ephesians 5:16. It's a commercial term. Seize the advantage, whenever it's given to you, to show by your life that the Christ way is the best way.

Then verse 6, *"Let your word be always with grace..."* "Speak graciously" we could translate it. When your walk is right then people will listen to your speech. That's why those two instructions go together under the heading of practice. Walk first then talk. It means observing the common courtesies of life. Speak graciously, "seasoned with salt." We sometimes say we take certain things with a pinch of salt, with doubt, yet Paul uses the figure in another way. He says to put a pinch of salt in everything you say, because salt has a seasoning value. Salt gives your words a lasting value; *"... seasoned with salt, to know how you ought to answer each one"* (verse 6b).

There's a beautiful passage in Matthew that says whenever you stand before kings for the sake of Christ, the words that you need to say *"will be given to you in that hour"* (Matthew 10:19). That is true in all of life's situations. When you come to that moment when God opens the door and you have the opportunity to say something, the answers you need will be there. And if you don't know the answer, do you know what you have to do? Be honest. Say "I don't know but I'll find out for you." Do not use that other slogan: "If you can't convince them, confuse them!" I believe God is available to give us answers at the moment we need them. God has that wisdom available to you and to me, so there's the practical side of the power of speech. Of course that does not excuse you from studying God's Word and remembering it. *"Always be prepared with a defence to everyone who asks you a reason for the hope that is in you, with meekness and fear"* (I Peter 3:15).

So let's review how we can use the power of speech. We can first pray, and we need to pray, to continue in prayer. Secondly, we can proclaim the truth, tell others about the good news as God opens that door of opportunity. Then, let's make sure we practice what we preach. We must be sure we get the walk right so that we have the talk right. Speech is a very powerful tool that God has given to us.

26

The Power of Christian Friends

Colossians 4:7-9

In the practical section of the letter to the Colossians, in chapters three and four, we've been learning how to get our lives straight. We now come to Paul's final greetings and those of his friends who were with him while he was under house arrest. You could be surprised by the valuable teaching that is in the last verses of this letter.

In verses 7 to 9 Paul talks about the two believers who carried the letter to the Colossians. It was his concern for other people that Paul wanted them to know of his condition, and so give comfort. *"Tychicus, the beloved brother and faithful minister, and fellow servant in the Lord, will tell you all things about me. [8]I am sending him to you for this very thing, that he may know your circumstances, and he may comfort your hearts, [9]with Onesimus, a faithful and beloved brother, who is one of you. They will make known to you all things here"* (verses 7-9). Tychicus and Onesimus were able to help Paul continue his ministry.

There is not a lot known about Tychicus. He was one of Paul's companions on his third missionary journey in Acts 20:4, and he is also mentioned as the bearer of the letter to the

Ephesian church in Ephesians 6:21. I will share the story of Onesimus in the last chapters of this book as we look at the letter to Philemon.

The Greek word for "comfort" (verse 8) is *"parakaleo,"* which means to call alongside. You call someone alongside to help you get you through a situation. When they come alongside they are there to help you. All of us have been in situations which we thought we couldn't handle ourselves. And of course that's quite true. We need God in partnership with us to solve the challenge, and we also have friends. We have fellow Christians, and we say to them, "I need to talk to someone about this." You call them alongside and you say, "Help me with this. How can I handle this situation? Pray with me for me guidance." They are there to help you going forward in that area.

Paul is under house arrest, he can't get about anymore, but he wants the Christians at Colossae to know that all is well with him. The power of speech is very powerful in this area of helping somebody else. Words can work wonders and words can work blunders. As it says in Ephesians in the parallel passage, words are *"good for edification* [building up], *that they may give grace to the hearers"* (Ephesians 4:29). So your words to somebody else, when you are called alongside, should build them up and help them to get their mind off the problem and on to God, so that life will be a lot easier for them.

You know, there's nothing more powerful than to just call up somebody to say, "I really appreciate you." We need to do a lot of that. Drop an email or a note to somebody you haven't written to for a long while and say, "Look, I really appreciate this, that, or the other" and just give them a little encouragement. Give them a lift because it will help them greatly. And later you may have the opportunity to be thankful somebody came along your side and said something to help you as well. So that's another usage of the power of speech—to help somebody else carry their burden, to encourage somebody else to exercise their faith in God and get on with the job of living God's way in a negative world.

Verses 10 to 18 of chapter 4 contain mention of more of Paul's Christian friends. There is a lot of power in having a bank of friends that you can draw on when you need it. John Donne wrote that "no man is an island, entire of itself." That means we all rub shoulders with other people. Other people's input can encourage or discourage our lives, and our comments and our actions can help their lives or drag them down. Our family gave us relatives, but God gave us friends. Would you like to change your relatives? Don't put your hands up! Our relatives are the "in-laws and the outlaws", as I call them. But we have friends, and there's nothing better than brothers and sisters in God's family that help give us a lift just when we need it.

Throughout Paul's fourteen writings he names well over a hundred people. These were his friends, fellow believers, or people he had met. Most were people he could count on. It's the same when I planned an overseas journey and would write to people along these lines, "If I came past your way, would you like me to stay with you for a couple of days?" Many of them would write back to say "Yes, anytime you want to come just say the word and you can always stay with us." It's good to have friends like that, isn't it? It ensures you don't feel lonely in a big country or a big city. So Paul named well over a hundred people, and as we come to this list of names in Colossians 4 we find that there are another eight people that get a mention. I want to really look at some of them carefully to see the power of Christian friends. Some of them stayed, some prayed, and one strayed.

27

Friends Who Stayed

Colossians 4:10-11, 14

The first group that I want to look at is the four friends whom Paul names as being fellow workers in the gospel and a comfort to him. The first one has a name that just rolls off the tongue, ***Aristarchus***. It's almost as good as Peter John! *"Aristarchus my fellow prisoner greets you"* (verse 10a). That's all it says about him in Colossians! The word means "the best ruler," and tradition makes him bishop of Assamea or Apamea in Syria. Here he gets just a brief mention, but it is quite interesting. Paul calls him a fellow prisoner or fellow captive. We are not sure whether he was actually a convicted person or awaiting trial like Paul was, or whether he simply volunteered to share Paul's imprisonment. I suspect he stayed with Paul because he knew Paul needed help. We understand that by the time the book of Colossians was written Paul was not languishing in a prison, but was detained in his own rented house (Acts 28:30) and chained to a soldier every day. Some of his friends would come to look after him and stay to take care of his needs, and Aristarchus was one of those.

Aristarchus gets a mention in Acts chapter 19. He was on a missionary journey with the apostle Paul (as was Tychicus) and they came to the city of Ephesus. In that city was the statue of the great goddess Diana, and there was also a trade union. You ought to read this chapter if you think we've got problems today. They had trade unions back in this time and they were even more violent than some are today. This united group of workers wanted to kill Paul and all his companions because their teaching about the God of love was affecting the worker's employment. Can you relate to that situation? In verse 29, *"And the whole city was filled with the confusion, and they rushed with one purpose into the theater, having seized Gaius and Aristarchus, Macedonians, travelling companions of Paul."* So we learn that Aristarchus, from Macedonia, was travelling with Paul and he was quite willing to get into the front line of the activities, and as a result was arrested. Verse 30, *"Now when Paul desired to enter into the people* [the crowd], *the disciples would not permit him."* Later on, in the next chapter, the party came to Greece and ministered for three months, and then Paul and a companion left for Macedonia while others, including Aristarchus, *"having gone ahead, were waiting for us in Troas"* (Acts 20:5).

Much later in the book of Acts, Paul is on his fourth journey which we call the voyage to Rome. It was on this voyage that he suffered a shipwreck on the island of Malta. Paul and Luke *"put to sea, Aristarchus, a Macedonian of Thessalonica, being with us"* (Acts 27:2). So Aristarchus went through riots with Paul. He went through shipwrecks with Paul, and when they finally got to Rome he decided to stay in the rented house with Paul and look after him. That's a good friend, isn't it? Aren't you glad there are people around like that who think enough of you that they support you through thick and thin? It's great to have friends who can be with you in the good times and be there when you really need them, when things are not going so well. Aristarchus was one who stayed. I appreciate people who've got some staying power about them because they believe what God is teaching them. They believe the positive "in Christ" approach to the Word of God and we need a lot more Aristarchus' who will bless us in that way.

The next person mentioned is *"Mark the cousin of Barnabas (about whom you received instructions: if he comes to you, receive him)"* (Colossians 4:10b). In other parts of the Bible he is called **John Mark,** and was the person who wrote the Gospel according to Mark. He was perhaps only a child when Jesus walked on the earth and the common view about his Gospel was that he spent a lot of time with Peter and obtained much information from him about the activities of Jesus. That's one viewpoint. I accept the viewpoint that God gave Mark the words to write and he did not need Peter's help. However, *"if he comes to you, receive* [welcome] *him."* The interesting thing about John Mark is that he went on the first missionary journey with Paul and Barnabas recorded in Acts 13 and 14. We don't know what part he played but *"they also had John* [Mark] *to assist them"* (Acts 13:5).

Then in Acts 15 we read of the humanity of the ministers of God, because Paul and Barnabas had an argument. Preachers are just as human as anybody else. *"And after some days Paul said to Barnabas, 'Let us return now and visit our brothers in each city where we proclaimed the word of the Lord, and see how they are doing.' 37Now Barnabas wanted to take with them John called Mark. 38But Paul insisted that they should not take with them one who had withdrawn from them in Pamphylia and had not gone with them to the work. ³⁹And there arose a sharp disagreement, so that they were separated from each other. Barnabas, taking along Mark, sailed to Cyprus"* (Acts 15:36-39). It appears that on that first missionary journey John Mark only went part of the way and then quit and went back to Jerusalem (Acts 13:13). Have you ever started something and then quit? "Quitters never win and winners never quit"—the motto of my athletic club, which is very true. But sometimes we do quit doing things, don't we? Sometimes we just feel that we can't continue with that action or concept. Well, John Mark quit. It doesn't tell us why he quit, just that he did. When they were getting ready to go out on the second missionary journey Paul made it clear there was no way he wanted a quitter on his team and he wouldn't take him. And Barnabas made it clear that if his cousin John Mark doesn't go, he was not going with Paul either. That's the kind of situation. And so they had an argument and John Mark went with Barnabas to Cyprus.

We don't read a lot more about him after this until we come here to Colossians and we find that he gets a mention. He's now one of the stayers. So even though there's been a relationship problem, now Paul and Mark get on well, and Mark sends his greetings to the Christians at Colossae. Paul commends him again in his second letter to Timothy, after Paul is released for a little while and then gets put back into prison again for the final time. Paul writes to Timothy, *"Luke alone is with me. Take Mark and bring him with you, for he is useful to me for ministry"* (II Timothy 4:11). So Mark goes from being a quitter to being "useful [helpful, profitable] to me for ministry". And that really tells us something.

There's someone in the Bible just like you and there's someone just like me, and we can learn from their victories and we can learn from their failures too. John Mark quit but he came back. John Mark failed but he was not a failure. Does that encourage you?

Some of you perhaps at times have decided that your faith in God doesn't work. It's a lot of trouble. You might be tempted to quit your faith for a little while. You might be tempted to throw it all away. "What's the good? I read my Bible every day. I've done this and that and it's not working." People, you may quit for a time but the Bible says that *"if we are faithless, He remains faithful; He* [Christ Jesus, verse 10] *cannot deny Himself"* (II Timothy 2:13). That's good isn't it? You may fail but you're not a failure. You may quit and say I've had enough for awhile but you are loved just the same as He loved you before. So can you learn something from John Mark? Yes, you certainly can. There are times when we quit but what we have to do is to pick up the pieces and get going again. John Mark was another stayer.

The next friend mentioned is *"Jesus who is called Justus"* (Colossians 4:11a). Jesus was common as a name in the days of the New Testament. It was a version of the Old Testament name Joshua and many males were called Jesus. In order to identify this man it uses the term "Jesus who is called Justus", so let's just call him ***Justus***. It has been suggested that his Jewish friends would call him Jesus, and his Greek and Roman friends would call him Justus. The record does not say much about him, except to group him with the men in the previous verse, *"... those being of the Circumcision* [Jews]. *These alone are my fellow workers for the kingdom of God, who have become a comfort to me"* (verse 11b).

They gave Paul the encouragement that he needed at that time. We read later in the letters to Timothy a list of the names of people who turned their back on Paul and no longer wanted to be associated with him and his positive ministry. Thank God for those who stayed! So Justus was another friend, another man who stayed, and in staying he was an encouragement, a comfort.

Are you getting the message from this that really one of the great reasons God has got you where you are is so that you can help the people you rub shoulders with? That's why you're there. It's to help the needs of humanity around you. I know the Bible teaches quite strongly that we should be concerned with the heathen in Africa and America and Australia and everywhere else, but it's the heathen next door and the heathen down the street and the heathen in your relatives that are your mission field. We are there to help them, and if you care for them then you have an opportunity to share the positive Word with them.

Another person is mentioned in this list of friends who looked after Paul, and that's in verse 14 where we read *"Luke the beloved physician greets you."* He is also mentioned in Philemon verse 24 and in II Timothy 4:11. *Luke* was the writer of the book of Acts as well as of the Gospel of Luke. Luke only mentions himself a couple of times in the book of Acts but we know when he was on the journeys with Paul because of the pronoun "we" that is used. I believe from about chapter 16 onwards he spent all his time with the apostle Paul.

Now in those days, as today, physicians were a very prosperous group of people in the community. Here is a physician, looked up to in the community, but it appears he set aside his

147

practice to travel with Paul. The apostle Paul had his own physician on the team and he was a Gentile. He was not Jewish in culture but he was one of those who stayed. So there are four friends who get special mention because they stayed with the apostle Paul: Three Jews—Aristarchus, John Mark, Justus—and one Gentile, Luke. They encouraged him. They looked after him. They helped him fulfill his ministry even though he was chained to a soldier every day.

28

Friends Who Prayed

Colossians 4:12-18

Colossians 4:12 mentions a man whose name is **Ephaphras** and he's known as the friend who prayed. *"Epaphras greets you, who is one of you..."*, so he was a Colossian. In fact, if you'll turn back to Colossians 1:7-8 you'll find that he gets a mention there as the man who brought Paul news of the Colossian church. *"Just as you learned from Epaphras, our beloved fellow servant, who is a faithful minister of Christ for you, ⁸who also told us of your love in the Spirit."* The word "learned" is the Greek word for "discipled." The Colossian believers were carefully discipled by Epaphras, who many believe started the church at Colossae.

"Ephaphras... a servant of Christ Jesus, always striving earnestly for you in his prayers, that you may stand mature and fully assured in all the will of God" (Colossians 4:12). So he was a man who prayed. Ephaphras perhaps could have spent his time praying to get out of prison. Philemon verse 23 says he was a fellow prisoner. Instead, he prayed for other people. His concern was this group of people that he had led to a knowledge of Christ Jesus and he wanted them to be mature in the faith and fully assured that God's will for them was health, wealth, and happiness. God's will

149

for you is set in concrete, and all your praying does not change His will but it does help you to be "fully assured" as to that will. That is a crucial point. Standing mature and fully assured go together. Ephaphras was a man who prayed.

"For I bear him witness that he has labored for you, and for those in Laodicea and in Hierapolis" (verse 13). There were three towns in the valley, and obviously Ephaphras had something to do with the work of God in all those three towns. So here was a friend who prayed, and he didn't just pray "Bless all the people everywhere." These verses say he prayed specifically for this group of believers. He prayed fervently and constantly. We can surmise that news of Paul's imprisonment had by now got back to other churches he had founded, and the believers in those churches would be praying for Paul and his travelling companions, now his fellow captives. Surely Paul would also count a good number of those believers as his friends too.

A friend who strayed

We've already mentioned verse 14, *"Luke the beloved physician greets you, as does Demas."* What about this man **Demas**? It doesn't say anything about him here except that he "greets you." There's no word of commendation about him. There's nothing said to identify him from anybody else apart from his name. I wonder why that is. There are clues in other books of the Bible. In the book of Philemon verses 23-24 we have some of these men mentioned that we've been looking at in this chapter: *"Epaphras, my fellow prisoner in Christ Jesus, sends greetings to you, and so do Mark, Aristarchus, Demas, and Luke, my fellow workers."* Demas gets a mention as one of Paul's fellow laborers. In II Timothy, written some years after Colossians, there is a third and final reference to this man. *"For Demas has forsaken me, having loved this present age, and gone to Thessalonica"* (II Timothy 4:10). Today we would probably say, "Demas has let me down."

Can you relate to that? Have you ever had friends that let you down? And what was the reason Demas let Paul down? It says he has loved this present age and has gone to Thessalonica. He walked out on Paul because he loved the lifestyle, the culture in which he lived. "This present age" is the world system. It's the culture, the society, the concepts, the way of thinking of the world. Demas loved the ease and comfort of the present age more than the sacrifice of serving God and Christ Jesus his Savior, and more than the great values that the Christian teaching had imparted to him. "Demas has let me down, deserted me, having loved this present age." He is the friend who strayed.

As you live and grow in Christ in a hostile world there will be some friends who perhaps are going to stray. It is still sad to lose a friend like that. Perhaps it may happen, but thank God for the friends we can count on—those who stay and the friends who pray. There's something very valuable about friendship, and when those friends are your brothers and sisters in the Christian faith they are of double value to you. So let's be very careful that we appreciate of all our friends.

Other friends

Only four verses of Colossians remain. *"Greet the brothers who are in Laodicea, and Nympha and the church in her house"* (Colossians 4:15). Here we have a church in the home of a lady, according to some manuscripts. Separate buildings for Christian worship did not appear until the third century. *"And when this letter has been read among you, have it also read in the church of the Laodiceans; and see that you also read the letter from Laodicea"* (verse 16). Whether the Laodicean letter has been lost we do not know. Some believe it refers to the letter to the Ephesians, because some manuscripts leave a blank in Ephesians 1:1 where the words "at Ephesus" appear in our English Bibles. So it could have been a circular letter that went first to Ephesus, then Laodicea, then Colossae. There are arguments for and against this theory.

"And say to Archippus, 'Take heed to the ministry that you have received in the Lord, that you fulfill it'" (verse 17). We can train a person to do positive Bible teaching but only God makes ministers. Archippus had a ministry that God had given to him, and Paul is encouraging him to keep on fulfilling it. In Philemon verse 2 Paul calls him his "fellow soldier."

"The greeting by my own hand, Paul. Remember my bonds. Grace be with you. Amen" (verse 18). Others had penned the letter that Paul had dictated, and now Paul, even though chained to a soldier, penned the last line, probably hearing the chains clinking as he wrote those words. Some texts have a note at the end, "To the Colossians, written from Rome by Tychicus and Onesimus."

29

A Letter to a Friend

Philemon 1-25

Once again I want to look into how to live and grow in Christ in a hostile world, and conclude this book on Colossians by sharing from the letter to Philemon. There is a very close association with this little book and the book of Colossians. Actually Philemon is the smallest of Paul's letters (that's why it is the last of 13 letters with Paul as the named writer), with only 445 words in 25 verses in the King James Version and only 335 words in the Greek text. It is, in effect, the only personal letter from the apostle Paul that we have. Paul wrote some deep teaching letters to churches. He also wrote letters to leaders of churches such as Timothy and Titus, but the book of Philemon is a personal letter to a friend. I think we are fortunate we have this because it illustrates how we can make practical this positive teaching of God's Word.

I have taught right through Colossians and shown you many principles. We discussed these under headings such as How to get the basics straight, How to get our heads straight, How to get our lives straight. Now when we come to Philemon, we see that the apostle Paul practiced what he preached. It's a beautiful little letter, full of some wonderful, powerful truths.

The background

Before we read Philemon, however, I'd like to remind you of one or two verses in Colossians. At the end of Colossians chapter 3 Paul had some words to say to those who were slaves. Let me remind you that half of the population of the Roman Empire were slaves. It was a very deep-rooted social condition. As slaves they had absolutely no rights whatsoever. The master was in total control. They had no right to get married, although the master sometimes kindly made available to them a permanent female companion and they lived in a family situation in many respects. The children born to that union were likewise slaves, and belonged totally to the master. If the master so desired he could punish the slaves, he could kill them, he could do whatever he wanted to them. Slaves were a "living tool."

Not once did the apostle Paul in any of his letters tell these slaves to revolt against the system. Not once did he tell them to go on strike. But he did have some very specific instructions on how to handle that area of life in which they were involved. In Colossians 3:22-23 he wrote, "*Slaves, obey in everything your masters according to the flesh, not by way of eye-service as people-pleasers, but in sincerity of heart, fearing the Lord.* [23]*Whatever you do, work heartily, as to the Lord and not to men, knowing that from the Lord you will receive the reward of the inheritance. Serve the Lord Christ.*" That was his instructions to slaves. He did not say to get out of the system. His attitude was that as a slave you are in the system, so do the best possible job you can. And not just when the master was looking but also when he's not around, because what you are doing is "to the Lord"—that is the critical thing.

Paul didn't just have words for the slaves. In Colossians 4:1 he had words to the masters, many of whom may have been cruel in their handling of the situation. Writing to masters who had become Christians, he said, "*Masters, give to your slaves what is just and fair, knowing that you also have a Master in heaven.*" Legally, masters did not have to give their slaves anything. They didn't even have to feed them if they did not want to. Yet God is saying to the masters, "give... what is just and fair." The word "give" there is also rendered to treat, to supply, to provide, out of your own prosperity. Give them what they need, what is right and fair. And on the other hand, slaves should give to their master the very best of their abilities.

In this way Christianity was at work within an oppressive system. This was because Christianity works on an individual basis, and if we can change individuals we will change our society. This is why the New Testament never speaks against the system of slavery, although it's quite obvious God's desire is that every person has the freedom and right to live their lives the way they want to. The New Testament does speak about changing individuals within a system, so that the system will eventually change, and it did!

Onesimus

In Colossians 4:9 we have a brief mention of a believer named Onesimus, "*the faithful and beloved brother, who is one of you.*" He came from the city of Colossae and was one of those sent by Paul to deliver his letters to the Colossian and Laodicean churches. Now let's go to the letter to Philemon, because we have in this small book the only other material known about this man

Onesimus. First I will briefly summarize the story as we are able to reconstruct it. It appears that Onesimus was a slave who belonged to Philemon, his master. In Philemon verse 18 Paul writes, *"If he has wronged you, or owes anything, charge that to my account."*

Onesimus had run away from his master after stealing something from him. Paul wrote in verse 15 that *"he was parted from you for a time."* Onesimus knew the cruelty of the masters of the day and he could well have lost his life because of his theft. And so he caught the next jet out of town. It's a familiar story of a runaway thief. He finished up in the city of Rome. Now Rome in Italy was a long way removed from Colossae, which was in Asia Minor, today's eastern Turkey. He would have gone through or around Greece into Italy, to get to Rome. In those ancient days it was a considerable distance.

Paul was chained to a soldier every day even though he lived in his own rented house. Somehow Onesimus, perhaps through a third person, was brought into Paul's house and he heard the good news of the gospel and became a Christian. *"I appeal to you for my child Onesimus, whom I have fathered in my imprisonment"* (verse 10). Now that changes everything, because this man was a thief but had now committed his life to Christ and was starting to learn how to live and grow in Christ in a hostile world. Perhaps none of us have had the problems that Onesimus had, because he knew that if he went back to Colossae to face his master he could be punished severely.

However, something else had also happened in the meantime. Philemon had also heard the good news. Now we believe that Philemon probably heard the gospel at Ephesus, and we can assume that a number of years have passed between when Onesimus ran away and when Paul led him to Christ in Rome. During that time Philemon had travelled the 100 miles from Colossae to Ephesus, where Paul (Acts 19:8-10) spent two and a quarter years telling people about the positive word of God. Philemon became a Christian, went back to Colossae and became a part of the local church in that city, which met in a house. So there are those two situations. Onesimus was saved in Rome and Philemon accepted Christ's offer of salvation probably in Ephesus and has gone back home.

30

Hearts Refreshed

Philemon 1-7

Now let's take this letter to Philemon from verse 1. It is a personal letter from Paul and it will be delivered to Philemon by the hand of Onesimus, a runaway slave and thief. On the journey Onesimus, along with others, is carrying the letter to the Colossians as well as the letter to the Laodiceans mentioned in Colossians 4:16. This is a very interesting situation.

"Paul, a prisoner of Christ Jesus, and Timothy our brother, to Philemon our beloved fellow worker, ²to our sister Apphia, and to Archippus our fellow soldier, and to the church in your house" (Philemon verses 1-2). So the Colossian church meetings were being held in Philemon's house. *"Grace to you and peace from God our Father, and the Lord Jesus Christ. ⁴I thank my God always, making mention of you in my prayers, ⁵hearing of your love and faith which you have toward the Lord Jesus and to all the saints"* (verses 3-5). Paul starts off positively and thanks God for the believers.

Now we come to verse 6. If you haven't got this verse underlined in your Bible or have a circle around it, please do so. I've taught on this verse many times and you'll find it elsewhere in my books. It is a powerful verse, so let's go into it in some depth. I usually quote it from the King James Version: *"That the communication of thy faith may become effectual by the acknowledging of every good thing which is in you in* [for] *Christ Jesus."* Other versions read, *"I pray that the sharing of your faith may become effective for the full knowledge of every good thing that is in us for the sake of Christ"* (ESV), *"...every good* [thing] *that is ours in* [our identification with] *Christ Jesus* [and unto His glory]*"* (Amplified), "There are numerous difficulties with the translation and interpretation of this verse" (NET Bible); read their footnotes for the details.

This is a powerful verse and is part of the reason why I like affirmations. The affirmation here is an acknowledgment of every good thing which is in you for Christ Jesus. I would like to first point out that this verse is not teaching that every good thing is in you. Rather, it is that every good thing is for the sake of Christ and only because you are in Christ do you become a recipient of all spiritual blessing. As we learned in Colossians 3:11, "Christ is all, and in all." Christ is preeminent in all things, and that includes "every good thing." In this sense verse 6 parallels the truth in another favorite verse of mine, Ephesians 1:3, where "every spiritual blessing" is "in Christ."

The next truth that needs to be understood is that your faith can be effective for you. The Amplified Bible reads "... your faith may produce"; "...may become operative" (Concordant); "...may become effective" (ESV). Having a faith and sharing it has to produce a benefit for God's kingdom and for you. How it becomes effective is now given.

The "acknowledging" or "recognition" is the key to the verse. The Greek word here means a thorough knowledge, in other words an experiential recognition. The NET Bible renders it as "may deepen your understanding." The Amplified uses the phrase a "full recognition and appreciation and understanding and precise knowledge." The Concordant uses the word "realization." This is the challenge that is facing perhaps 90 per cent of Christians today. Most do not know to any depth that they are blessed with every spiritual blessing, and while a small number talk about it, only a minority enjoy an "experiential recognition" of their position and possessions. Now perhaps you are getting a glimpse of the depth and impact of the truth in this verse. *"For the sake of Christ Jesus."* It is all for His glory, not yours! Meditate on it and drill it into your consciousness that you do have and can enjoy "every good thing... for Christ Jesus."

"For we have great joy and comfort over your love, because the hearts of the saints are refreshed by you, brother" (verse 7). Now Paul thanks Philemon for helping the believers.. "Hearts... refreshed"; what a great testimony to the practical Christianity of Philemon. The word "refreshed" is from the same root word as used by Jesus in Matthew 11:28 when he said, *"Come to me, all who labor and are heavy laden, and I will give you rest* [rejuvenation]." The phrase is also used in Paul's appeal to Philemon in verse 20. The U.S. army term "R&R", Rest and Recuperation, has come into common usage, though there is no agreement on what words the initials really stand for. Every believer needs time to be refreshed in their heart, the seat of the personal life. This is not a new anointing or a fresh touch from the Lord or a refilling of the Spirit, but some kindness or example in word or deed from a fellow believer. Refresh someone's heart today!

31

Paul's Appeal to Philemon

Philemon 8-25

"Therefore, having much boldness in Christ to command you to do what is fitting, ⁹*yet for love's sake I appeal to you—I, Paul the aged, and now a prisoner also of Christ Jesus"* (verses 8-9). Paul was getting on in years, probably being in the mid-50s or so at this point, and most translations speak of "Paul the aged." Life expectancy was much lower then than it is today. Culturally because of his age, respect from others was called for, somewhat different from today. Note the "in Christ" in verse 8, the first of five usages in Philemon.

"I appeal to you for my child Onesimus, whom I have fathered in my imprisonment" (verse 10). Paul calls Onesimus his child because he fathered him in the Christian faith. Paul is saying, "Even though I am bound here in Rome, I've brought in this new family member. I have introduced this man Onesimus into God's family." Every name has a meaning, as you are well aware. The name Peter means "a rock," for example. The name Onesimus means "profitable" or "useful." There is a play on that word in verse 11, *"who once was useless to you, but now is useful to you and to me."* Certainly when he stole from his master he became quite unprofitable. In fact,

he ran off with the profits! But "now is useful to you and to me." When Onesimus found God and Christ came into his life, he became profitable, useful to both Paul and Philemon.

"Whom I am sending back to you. You then receive him, that is, my very heart; [13]*whom I wished to keep with myself, in order that on your behalf he might serve me in the bonds of the gospel,* [14]*But I wished to do nothing without your consent, in order that your good might not be of compulsion, but willingly"* (verses 12-14). Paul is not appealing to Philemon to give Onesimus his freedom. As always, Paul did not attack the social structure of his day, but he is appealing for Philemon to voluntarily make Onesimus available to him again. He wanted the situation of a thief and his master to be resolved, so he is sending Onesimus back to face the music. If ever I have to face the music for a crime, I sure would want someone like the apostle Paul to write a letter like this, wouldn't you?

"For perhaps he was taken away for a time, in order that you might keep him forever, [16]*no longer as a slave but above a slave—a beloved brother especially to me, yet how much more to you, both in the flesh and in the Lord"* (verses 15-16). What a beautiful statement. He left for a little while but now I'm sending him back, and because you belong to the family of God and Onesimus belongs to the family of God, you have him forever. From a slave to a sibling! In the culture still a slave, but in reality a brother for eternity. He stole from you but love him anyway, because now you are both in the same family.

"If then you count me as a partner, receive him as me" (verse 17). Philemon really didn't have a lot of choices, and that is what Paul is reminding him. "Look, if you love God, you should take this

man back. You should forgive him for what he's done, and from now on you will have a different relationship. Sure, he will still be a slave and you will still be a master, but you are now brothers in the same family and so you can work together on a higher plane."

Verse 18 is another powerful verse in the letter to Philemon. *"But if he has wronged you, or owes you anything, charge that to me."* What a beautiful statement! "Put that on my account" (NKJV). Some of my readers can relate to that. You stand at the door of the department store like a knight on a white horse and holler "Charge!" Charge it to my account.

"I, Paul, wrote this with my own hand: I will repay it, lest I say to you that even yourself you owe to me" (verse 19). Paul often used a secretary to write down his words, but this personal letter he wrote with his own hand. Many believe these statements go beyond just a personal letter from Paul to Philemon. Luther wrote, "We are all His Onesimi, to my thinking." The account is a reflection of God's love for us as His children. Jesus came to this earth to pay the debt that you and I should have paid for our sins. We were the ones who ran away from God, yet Jesus came to pay that debt. It says in Romans 5:10 that *"... while we were enemies we were reconciled to God by the death of his Son."* While we were acted like His enemies, He loved us and paid the debt for us. He knew we had done wrong but He still said "charge it to my account."

Jesus paid it all. It's a beautiful illustration of the gospel truth. There was absolutely nothing that we could do about our situation but Jesus paid it all, and because He paid it we now are in the family of God. We now have fellowship with God once again. It is a powerful verse, not only from the viewpoint of Paul and Philemon in relation to Onesimus, but also from the viewpoint of Christ Jesus and God in relation to you and to me. "He paid a debt He did not owe, I owed a debt I could not pay..." as one chorus so beautifully expresses the truth.

And then verse 20, *"Yes, brother, may I have profit from you in the Lord; refresh my heart in the Lord."* Philemon refreshed the hearts of others (verse 7), now Paul asks him to refresh his heart. The King James Version renders the word "profit" as "joy" but the word means "useful, profitable" and is from the same root word as the name "Onesimus." So Paul is saying, "Here is this man named Profitable. I'm sending him back to you. Now you let me have some profit because of this situation. Let me be blessed because how you are going to handle this situation, Philemon. Refresh my heart in the Lord. I will be really blessed to see you and Onesimus getting on together once again."

Now Paul takes it a step further, *"Having confidence in your obedience, I write to you, knowing that you will do above what I say"* (verse 21). Isn't that great? "More than I say." And it's the same with Jesus Christ. He died for our sins, but He did more than that. He not only provided salvation from the power and penalty of sin but he also died for my health as well. He also died for my prosperity. He also died that I might enjoy life to the very full. He went beyond just paying the penalty of sin. He died that I might have "life more abundantly" (John 10:10).

The next verse in Philemon contains a faith statement, an affirmation of Paul as to his desire to do more work in the church. *"Now, at the same time, make ready also a lodging for me, for I am expecting that, through your prayers, I shall be freely given to you"* (verse 22). He wrote a similar statement to the Philippian believers from the same imprisonment (Philippians 2:24). Some commentators believe he did get his freedom for a few more years before he was imprisoned again.

Finally, Paul names the same people that are named at the end of the book of Colossians. *"Epaphras, my fellow prisoner in Christ Jesus, greets you, 24as so do Mark, Aristarchus, Demas, and Luke, my fellow workers. 25The grace of the Lord Jesus Christ be with your spirit, Amen"* (Philemon 23-25). The letter starts with "grace" (verse 3), demonstrates grace in action throughout, and concludes with "grace" (verse 25).

If tradition is correct, Onesimus went on to become a good minister and then a bishop in the early church. Later, he was imprisoned in Rome and martyred by stoning (although some sources claim that he was beheaded). Yet it is enough to see at this point of time that Onesimus found Christ, and Philemon found Christ, and even though they had a difference of opinion over some material possessions, they were able to sort it out because both men had Christ in their heart. With the help of the apostle Paul's encouragement, I believe they did sort it out and went on to live profitable lives.

So what can we learn from Philemon on how to live and grow in Christ in a hostile world? We've learned that it's not just a matter of being positive mentally, and it's not just a matter of being positive with our speech. We also need to be positive in practical ways. It is possible to make God's Word work. It's possible to make it work in family situations, in marriage situations, in business situations. In fact, it works in every situation.

God has never asked us to do anything it's impossible for us to do. If God said we can live His way in a hostile world, then we can do it. Each one of you can do it because you have the positive One within you. You are not on your own. It is God in Christ in you. It is you and God working on life's situations, and with that kind of partnership then every one of us can live the way God planned for us.

Last Words

The book is finished. Our journey of inspiration through both Colossians and Philemon has come to an end, for the present. I feel sure you will want to dip into its pages again, for it is loaded with so much truth that very few of us can take it in on our first reading. If you have read it straight through, go back and read a chapter a day. If on the other hand you have read a chapter a day, start reading it again at your own pace. You will be amazed at what you discover on your second time through.

Perhaps you have grasped for the first time the absolute centrality of Christ in all things, including your religion. Christ is mentioned by name 26 times in Colossians. Hopefully you will have been encouraged to deepen your relationship with your Lord and Savior. Now you know that you need to *"grow up into him in all things,"* as Ephesians 4:15 puts it. In these politically correct times of relativism, it is refreshing to have some absolutes that provide a solid foundation for everyday life.

Share these truths with your Christian friends. Sit down and discuss what the Word actually says. Encourage others to get their own copy of this book and to read it often. Send us an email or write to us and share your blessings.

Index of Scriptures

168

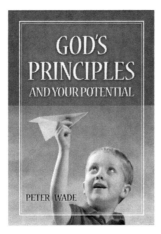

Also by Peter Wade

GOD'S PRINCIPLES AND YOUR POTENTIAL

EXPLORING THE MYTH OF A CAPRICIOUS GOD AND RELEASING THE POTENTIAL OF EVERY BELIEVER

God's spiritual principles are constant and unchanging. When we apply them with confidence, positive Christian living becomes a reality for us. The great men and women of Bible days learned these truths, and you can also learn them from God's Word.

It will come as a surprise to many Christians that God is not a God of capriciousness but a God of principle. We can rely on God to fulfill His Word always. This truth takes the strain and stress out of Christian living, and makes it an exciting adventure.

Here are nine principles clearly explained by the author, who has taught the Bible for over 50 years. The final two principles are amplified in greater detail in Parts 2 and 3 of the book.

ISBN 9780909362317

Available now from online booksellers, and full details are online at **www.PeterWade.com/principles/**

Quantity prices available on all our titles!

Also by Peter Wade

SEEDS AND SECRETS

CULTIVATING GOD'S SEEDS OF GREATNESS AND APPLYING GOD'S SECRETS OF SUCCESS TO BECOME VICTORS, NOT VICTIMS

There has never been a greater need in Christian circles than now to re-examine God's plan for His family. First, this book looks at the Genesis record and demonstrates that God placed in Adam seeds of greatness that are our inheritance.

Then chapter 8 covers the record of the 12 spies unnecessary journey into the Promised Land. In the following 8 chapters God's command to Joshua is used as a foundation for teaching God's secrets of success.

You will learn also that you are IN-dependent when you have Christ within, not co-dependent on others. You really can be a victor, not a victim.

ISBN 9780909362294

Available now from online booksellers, and full details are online at **www.PeterWade.com/seeds/**

Also available in **Spanish** as *Semillas y Secretos*

Edited by Peter Wade

In Christ TREASURES

19th CENTURY PULPIT GREATS ON "IN CHRIST" TRUTH,
Including A.J. GORDON, ANDREW MURRAY,
A.J. PIERSON, A.B. SIMPSON, AND OTHERS

Nine great teachers from the past... all in one book to inspire, challenge and guide you! These teachers were all household names in their day, all were successful pastors, missionaries, or academics. They came from different denominations and movements... yet all were captivated by just two words in the Word of God: "In Christ".

This valuable collection contains two complete books and nine significant chapters from great preachers of the 19th century, totalling 47 chapters in all, plus Peter Wade's complete concordance of "In Christ" scriptures, both by form and book order. There is no other work on the market with so much specific "In Christ" teaching as this new volume.

ISBN 9780909362331

Available now from online booksellers, and full details are online at **www.PeterWade.com/treasures/**

También por Peter Wade
LA DINÁMICA DEL
VIVIR POSITIVO

La Biblia solo revela La provisión de Dios para la vida del creyente, y en la medida en que usted ajuste su pensamiento a la verdad, usted podrá ahondar en Sus recursos para una vida positiva y próspera.

Los quince grandes capítulos de este libro lo inspirarán a verse ¡como bendito con lo mejor del Cielo! ¿Por qué vivir por debajo cuando lo mejor está disponible para usted? Usted tiene el poder para enfrentar cada situación en que se encuentre, y salga victorioso cada vez.

ISBN 9780909362300

Disponible en la librería en línea, o consiga todos los detalles en línea en **www.PeterWade.com/vivirpositivo/**

EN CRISTO:
UNA NUEVA CREACIÓN

Este desafiante y positivo libro dará una fresca mirada a que Dios nos ha hecho estar en Cristo. Los cristianos no necesitan sentirse indignos, no necesitan mendigar y suplicar, ellos no necesitan mas resistir de disfrutar todas las bendiciones de Dios.

En este inspirador libro, tu descubrirás que entender en el Nuevo Testamento el concepto de una nueva creación traerá satisfacción, la oración será revitalizada, los milagros se volverán normales y la guía de Dios será reconocida y aplicada, en el capitulo final le enseñará como volverse un cristiano, una nueva creación en Cristo.

ISBN 9780909362324

Disponible en la librería en línea, o consiga todos los detalles en línea en **www.PeterWade.com/resources/**

OTHER POSITIVE BOOKS BY PETER WADE

In Christ: A New Creation This challenging and positive book that takes a fresh look at what God has made us to be in Christ. No longer need Christians feel unworthy; no longer need they beg and plead, no longer need they hold back from enjoying all of God's blessings. You will see that understanding the Biblical concept of a New Creation will bring contentment, prayer will be revitalized, miracles will become normal, and God's guidance will be recognized and acted upon.

48 pages, large format paperback. ISBN 978 0 909362 27 0

Exciting Ephesians Thrill to the truth of this exciting revelation of God to man. The author's excitement for what one scholar has called "God's highest and best" epistle will encourage you to dig deeper into Paul's letter to the Ephesians. This book is a journey of exploration and inspiration, not just a commentary. It presents highlights of this powerful letter from the viewpoint of the New Creation and the Christ-life within each believer.

128 pages, large format paperback. ISBN 978 0 909362 23 2

Outdo, Outwit & Outperform A rich blend of motivational and inspirational material for business and personal life, practical not preachy, while firmly based on the Bible. Christianity was always intended to be a practical way of life, rather than a ritualistic religion. Ten "How to..." chapters with intensely practical ways to fully express the Christ within you.

96 pages, large format paperback. ISBN 978 0 909362 24 9

Four Keys to Prosperity God's prosperity plan for believers is brought to light in a practical yet profound manner in this book. The balanced scriptural exposition uses the four keys to depict the mental and spiritual laws of prosperity. The four chapters are ideal for both personal reading and group study. Includes eight one-page mini-posters of significant prosperity verses and an index to the scriptures quoted, wrapped in a silk-embossed brilliant gold cover. Learn how to operate these four keys and get into the flow of God's prosperity.

64 pages, large format paperback. ISBN 978 0 909362 22 5

While stocks last — **www.PeterWade.com/resources/**

CPSIA information can be obtained at www.ICGtesting.com
Printed in the USA
LVOW06s0708151213

365373LV00001B/103/P